The Grass Grows Where I Am

NOAH CRANE

18 Holistic Experts Share Wisdom and Tools to Empower Your Life Beyond Your Wildest Dreams

Published by:
World Healing Tour
BOCA RATON, FL

In association with:
The Grass Grows Where I Am: With Noah Crane
CEO World Healing Tour Collective & Expo
2025 President Boca Raton Holistic Chapter
Spotify Podcast Host: Heal Yourself, Heal the World

Copyright © 2026 Noah Crane

All rights reserved.

ISBNs:
Softcover (B&W): 978-1-7331728-1-3
Softcover (Color): 978-1-7331728-2-0
Ebook: 978-1-7331728-3-7

Disclaimer: This publication is strictly an informational and educational resource, intended only to share general information, wisdom, and ideas. The content provided is not a substitute for personalized professional advice; it does not constitute or offer medical, mental health, legal, financial, or any other type of professional counseling. Because every situation is unique, readers must always consult with a qualified professional who can assess their individual circumstances before acting on any information presented. The publisher does not endorse any specific method or concept. By using this publication, you acknowledge that the creators, publishers, and distributors of this content will not be held liable for any decisions made or actions taken based on the information provided.

*This book is dedicated to every one of the authors
in this heart-centered collaboration.*

*Thank you for your commitment to personal growth,
for saying yes to yourselves, and for your dedication
to leaving this world a better place for all.*

Growth Pillars

WORTHINESS
Christine Abrahams
Noah Crane
Carrie Leskowitz

RESILIENCE
Sonia Artwell
Leslie Carmen
Lynn Lessell
Abbey Jo Shulkin
Tina Vaida
Tami Lynn Wellman

ENLIGHTENMENT
Dr. Samantha Carney
Clive Digby-Jones
Dr. Daniel Hulsey
Ricki Moskow

WISDOM
Susan Brauser
Dr. Kathy Brooks Holloway
Dr. Steven Crane
Diana M. Drake
Ester Mizrahi

Contents

Introduction..1
A Personal Note for You from Noah Crane

WORTHINESS

Finding Worthiness in Label-Free Parenting............ 18
Christine Abrahams, EdD, NCC, LPC, LMHC, ACS

You Are Not Broken! You Are Enough!
Believe in You!...34
Noah Crane

Cultivating Your Space, Affirming Your
Worthiness..50
Carrie Leskowitz

RESILIENCE

Women's Wisdom: Nurturing Resilience
Through Mind, Body & Spirit................................68
Sonia Artwell

Trigeminal Neuralgia: The Cost of Silence
& the Resilient Fight for Life 84
Leslie Carmen

From Stressed to Resilience 102
Lynn Lessell

From Binge to Balance: A Life Shift in Recovery 116
Abbey Jo Shulkin

Empowering Women and Children:
Wisdom, Strength, and Global Impact 132
Tina Vaida

Cultivating a Garden of Faith:
Thriving Where You're Planted 146
Tami Lynn Wellman

ENLIGHTENMENT

A Journey of Wisdom and Enlightenment:
Biohacking Chiropractic Care 160
Dr. Daniel Hulsey & Dr. Samantha Carney

The Art of Cultivating a Whole Human—
the Missing Peace 176
Clive Digby-Jones

Name It, Frame It & Claim It 192
Ricki Moskow

WISDOM

Cellular Hydration Holds the Key to Radiant
Health, Smart and Simple! 208
Susan Brauser

The Earth's Whisper: A Journey of Wisdom
and Resilience 224
Dr. Kathy Brooks Holloway

Peace or Frustration: The Choice Is Yours 240
Dr. Steven Crane, DMD

Thyroid & Hormone Healing Power:
Wisdom Gained with Homeopathy
and Natural Herb Protocols................................256
Diana M. Drake, PhD

The Wisdom of Nonnegotiables.......................... 270
Ester Mizrahi

Acknowledgments 282

About the Anthologist 283
Noah Crane #1 Bestselling Author and CEO

Introduction

A Personal Note for You from Noah Crane

Welcome, dear friend, to the verdant landscape of the co-author experience we collectively call, *The Grass Grows Where I Am*. Your arrival here is no mere coincidence; it is a moment ordained, a juncture in your journey where the seeds of self-reflection and profound discovery are ready to be sown. We, the co-authors of this literary endeavor, extend our deepest gratitude and heartfelt honor for your presence within these pages. In this shared space, we wish to highlight the essence of our collective spirit, a sentiment both simple and profound: This co-author book is a voyage into the depths of your being, a guided exploration led by voices steeped in the wisdom of worthiness, the strength of resilience, the illumination of enlightenment, and the grounded wisdom of lived experience. Each of us carries a narrative uniquely shaped by the contours of our individual lives. Yet, within these diverse tapestries of experience, a common thread binds us—the unwavering belief in the inherent potential that resides within every human heart. Our aim is to ignite within you a *spark of recognition, to inspire and motivate* you to delve into the wellspring of your own inner strength, to unearth the boundless possibilities that lie dormant within, and to seize the reins of your own destiny with courage and conviction. This journey encourages you to embrace the exquisite mosaic of your unique gifts and qualities, to navigate the inevitable storms of life with fortitude, and to fearlessly pursue the passions and dreams that whisper to your soul.

Within these chapters, you will find a wealth of insight and practical strategies carefully cultivated to nurture the seeds of self-confidence, foster an unyielding resilience, and illuminate the path toward a profound sense of purpose. Ultimately, the very heart of this book beats with a singular intention: to empower you to live authentically, to embrace transformative change, and to cultivate a life that resonates with meaning and purpose, not only for yourself, but also for the intricate web of relationships that enrich your existence—your children, your partners, your cherished friends, and your beloved family.

Before you embark further into this unfolding narrative, we implore you to pause, to draw a breath, and to truly acknowledge the magnificent being that you already are. You stand as a radiant beacon of light in this world, imbued with a remarkable capacity for growth and an insatiable curiosity. Within you lies divine gifts and singular talents yearning to be expressed, and the world stands in profound need of their illumination now more than ever before.

The creation of this book has been a transformative process for each of us, a journey mirroring the very essence of life itself—a dynamic interplay of energizing moments, exhilarating discoveries, and deeply rewarding connections. We, the co-authors, have converged as a unified collective, our individual voices harmonizing in a symphony of co-creation, guided by the singular intention of serving the greatest and highest good of all. Each contributor embarked on this mission with a shared vision: to collaborate and connect through the profound act of sharing the deep insights gleaned from their own personal odysseys of resilience—that remarkable capacity to recover swiftly from life's inevitable difficulties, that inherent toughness that allows the spirit to spring back into vibrant form, unbent and unbroken.

As you turn these pages, you will encounter the raw vulnerabilities, the authentic lived experiences, and the impassioned voices of each author who has poured their heart and soul into this thought-provoking and masterful body of work. Each one carries a fervent desire to leave an indelible mark, however subtle or grand, upon the tapestry of the world. It is our most profound and heartfelt wish that you step into the next chapter of your life's unfolding story armed with newfound tools of empowerment, skills that will serve as unwavering companions as you tap into the wellspring of your own masterful life work.

We envision you living in the radiant embrace of your own love and light, sharing your unique constellation of gifts with the world without the shadow of comparison, the sting of competition, or the constricting fear of scarcity. This unwavering belief in abundance and interconnectedness is a cornerstone shared among all the co-collaborators of this endeavor. We stand united in the conviction that our achievable goal is to continue lifting one another, to celebrate one another's triumphs, and to contribute to the collective elevation of all. For in this shared journey, we wholeheartedly believe, "Together We Are Won."

Now, let us delve deeper into the foundational pillars that underpin this transformative journey of self-discovery, the very essence of *The Grass Grows Where I Am: Worthiness, Resilience, Enlightenment, and Wisdom*. Each of these pillars represents a crucial aspect of your inner landscape, a vital element in cultivating a life that is not only meaningful but also deeply fulfilling and authentically your own.

The First Pillar: Worthiness
The Unshakeable Foundation of Self

The journey toward a flourishing life invariably begins with the profound and unwavering recognition of one's own inherent worthiness. This is not a quality to be earned or acquired through external validation; rather, it is an intrinsic truth, a birthright bestowed upon every soul that graces this earth. To truly believe in one's worthiness is to lay down an unshakeable foundation upon which all other aspects of a fulfilling life can be built. Without this fundamental belief, the seeds of self-doubt and insecurity can take root, hinder growth, and obscure the brilliance of one's true potential.

Worthiness is the quiet knowing within that you are inherently valuable, deserving of love, respect, happiness, and all the good that life has to offer, abundance simply because you exist. It is the internal compass that guides you toward self-compassion and self-acceptance, even in the face of imperfections and mistakes. When you operate from a place of deep-seated worthiness, you are less likely to seek external validation or allow the opinions of others to define your sense of self-worth. Instead, your value emanates from within, a steady and unwavering light that illuminates your path.

Exploring the depths of worthiness requires a gentle yet courageous introspection. Often, societal conditioning, past experiences, and negative self-talk can erode this innate sense of value. We may have internalized messages that suggest we are not good enough, not smart enough, not capable enough. The journey back to worthiness involves consciously challenging these limiting beliefs, dismantling the internal critic, and cultivating a compassionate inner dialogue of self-love. When your inner critic comes in, put some light on it.

Practically cultivating worthiness involves several key steps:

- Self-Awareness: Begin by becoming acutely aware of your thoughts and beliefs about yourself. Identify the negative or limiting narratives that play on repeat in your mind. Question their validity and origin. Are these truly your own beliefs, or are they echoes of past experiences or external influences?

- Self-Compassion: Treat yourself with the same kindness and understanding that you would offer a dear friend facing difficulties. Acknowledge your imperfections as part of human experience and extend grace toward yourself when you stumble.

- Setting Boundaries: Recognizing your worth empowers you to establish healthy boundaries in your relationships and interactions. It allows you to say "no" to demands that feel draining or disrespectful and to prioritize your own well-being.

- Celebrating Your Strengths: Focus on acknowledging and celebrating your unique talents, skills, and positive qualities. Make a conscious effort to recognize your accomplishments, no matter how small they may seem. Learn to celebrate you.

- Affirmations and Positive Self-Talk: Consciously replace negative self-talk with positive affirmations and encouraging inner dialogue. Remind yourself of your inherent value and capabilities on a regular basis.

- Mindfulness and Presence: Cultivating mindfulness allows you to be present in the moment, appreciating yourself and your experiences without judgment. It helps to quiet the noise of self-criticism and fosters a sense of inner peace.

- Seeking Supportive Connections: Surround yourself with people who uplift and affirm your worth. Healthy relationships are built on mutual respect and appreciation, reinforcing your sense of value.

The journey to reclaiming and embodying your inherent worthiness is not always linear. There will be moments of doubt and old patterns may resurface. However, with consistent self-awareness, compassion, and intentional effort, you can cultivate an unshakeable belief in your own value, paving the way for a life lived with greater confidence, joy, and authenticity. When you truly believe you are worthy, you open yourself up to receive the abundance and fulfillment that life has to offer, recognizing that you deserve all that is good in our world.

The Second Pillar: Resilience
The Art of Bending Without Breaking

Life, in its intricate dance of joy and sorrow, inevitably presents us with challenges, obstacles, setbacks, and moments of profound difficulty. It is in these times that the second crucial pillar, resilience, becomes our steadfast anchor. Resilience is not about avoiding hardship or being immune to pain; rather, it is the remarkable capacity to navigate adversity, to adapt to change, and to bounce back from setbacks with renewed strength and purpose. It is the inner fortitude that allows us to bend in the face of the storm without breaking, to learn from our experiences, and to emerge from the crucible of challenge not diminished but strengthened.

Resilience is not a fixed trait but rather a dynamic process that can be cultivated and strengthened over time. It involves a complex interplay of personal resources, coping mechanisms, and a positive mindset. Individuals who exhibit high levels of resilience often possess a strong sense of self-efficacy, believing in their ability to influence events and overcome obstacles. They tend to be optimistic, possess effective problem-solving skills, and have a strong support network to draw upon during difficult times.

Developing resilience is an active and ongoing process. Here are some key strategies for cultivating this vital inner strength:

- Cultivating a Growth Mindset: Embrace the belief that your abilities and intelligence can be developed through dedication and hard work. View challenges not as fixed limitations but as opportunities for learning and growth.

- Developing Emotional Regulation Skills: Learn to recognize and manage your emotions effectively, particularly during times of stress. Practice techniques such as mindfulness, deep breathing, and self-soothing to navigate difficult feelings without being overwhelmed.

- Building Strong Support Networks: Nurture meaningful relationships with family, friends, and mentors who provide emotional support, encouragement, and a sense of belonging. Lean in on these connections during challenging times.

- Practicing Self-Care: Prioritize your physical, emotional, and mental well-being through activities that nourish your mind, body, and spirit. This includes adequate sleep, healthy eating, regular exercise, and engaging in activities you enjoy daily.

- Developing Problem-Solving Skills: Cultivate your ability to analyze challenges, identify potential solutions, and take proactive steps to address them. Break down large problems into smaller, more manageable steps.

- Finding Meaning and Purpose: Connecting with something larger than yourself, whether it's through your work, your values, or your spiritual beliefs, can provide a sense of meaning and purpose that helps you navigate adversity with greater resilience.

- Learning from Past Experiences: Reflect on past challenges and identify the lessons learned and the strengths you developed in overcoming them. This can build confidence in your ability to handle future difficulties.

- Practicing Optimism: Cultivate a hopeful outlook and focus on the positive aspects of a situation, even amid challenges. While it's important to acknowledge difficulties, maintaining a sense of possibility can fuel your resilience.

- Acceptance and Adaptability: Recognize that change is an inevitable part of life and develop the ability to adapt to new circumstances with flexibility and grace. Learn to let go of what you cannot control or change.

- Grit: Resilience is not about being invincible; it's about having the inner resources to navigate the inevitable storms of life, to learn and grow from them, and to emerge with a deeper understanding of yourself and the world around you. It is the quiet strength that allows the grass to bend in the wind, knowing that it will rise again, stronger, greener, and more deeply rooted.

The Third Pillar: Enlightenment
Illuminating the Path to Understanding

The third pillar, enlightenment, speaks to the profound human yearning for understanding, for insight, and for a deeper connection to yourself, to others, and to the world around you. It is the process of shedding illusions, of gaining clarity, and of awakening to a more expansive and truthful perception of reality. Enlightenment is not necessarily a sudden, dramatic event but rather an ongoing journey of intellectual, emotional, and spiritual growth. Enlightenment involves a relentless pursuit of knowledge, a willingness to question assumptions, and an openness to new perspectives. It is about moving beyond superficial understanding and delving into the deeper currents of truth that underline our experiences. This pillar encourages you to cultivate curiosity, to engage in critical thinking, and to seek wisdom from diverse sources. The path to enlightenment can take many forms, including:

- Intellectual Exploration: Engaging with books, articles, lectures, and other sources of information to expand your understanding of various subjects, from science and philosophy to art and history.

- Introspection and Self-Inquiry: Turning your gaze inward to examine your own thoughts, beliefs, and emotions. Through practices like meditation and journaling, you can gain deeper self-awareness and identify limiting patterns and beliefs.

- Learning from Diverse Perspectives: Actively seeking out and engaging with viewpoints that differ from your own. This can challenge your assumptions and broaden your understanding of complex issues and situations.

- Cultivating Empathy and Compassion: Striving to understand the experiences and perspectives of others, fostering a sense of interconnectedness to all and reducing your own judgments.

- Spiritual Exploration: Engaging in practices that connect you to something larger than yourself, whether through religion, spirituality, or a deep appreciation for the natural world around you.

- Creative Expression: Engaging in artistic pursuits that allow you to explore and communicate with your inner world, fostering new insights and perspectives.

- Mindfulness and Presence: Cultivating the ability to be fully present in the moment, observing your thoughts and experiences without judgment, which can lead you to profound insights and more clarity.

- Experiential Learning: Embracing new experiences and stepping outside your comfort zone, allowing you to learn and grow through direct engagement with the world around you.

Enlightenment is not about achieving a state of perfect knowledge or absolute certainty. Rather, it is a continuous process of seeking, questioning, and evolving your understanding. It is about cultivating a mind that is open, curious, and receptive to new information and perspectives. As you gain greater clarity and insight, you are better equipped to navigate the complexities of life, make informed decisions, and live in alignment with your deepest values and desires. The light of enlightenment illuminates the path forward, guiding you toward a more meaningful and fulfilling existence.

The Fourth Pillar: Wisdom
The Fruit of Experience and Reflection

The final pillar, wisdom, represents the culmination of your journey through worthiness, resilience, and enlightenment. It is the profound understanding that arises from the integration of knowledge, experience, and reflection. Wisdom is not simply about accumulating information; it is about discerning truth, making sound judgments, and acting with compassion and insight. It is the ability to apply your understanding in a way that benefits yourself and the world around you. Wisdom is often associated with maturity and life experience, but it is not solely a function of age. It is cultivated through a conscious process of learning from your experiences, both successes and failures, and reflecting deeply upon their meaning. Wise individuals possess a balanced perspective, recognizing the interconnectedness of all things and acting with foresight and empathy. Cultivating wisdom involves:

- Reflection and Introspection: Taking time to thoughtfully consider your experiences, your actions, and their consequences. Asking yourself what you have learned and how you can apply those lessons moving forward.

- Learning from Mistakes: Viewing failures not as defeats but as valuable opportunities for growth and learning. Extracting the lessons embedded within challenging experiences and times.

- Seeking Mentorship and Guidance: Learning from the wisdom of those who have walked the path before you. Engaging with mentors and seeking guidance from experienced individuals.

- Practicing Empathy and Compassion: Cultivating the ability to understand and share the feelings of others, and acting with kindness, love, and consideration.

- Developing Discernment: Learning to distinguish between what is true and false, important and trivial. Making sound judgments based on insight and understanding.

- Living in Alignment with Values: Acting in accordance with your deepest held principles and beliefs, ensuring that your actions are congruent with your values.

- Cultivating Patience and Acceptance: Recognizing the cyclical nature of life and embracing the present moment with equanimity.

- Sharing Knowledge and Experience: Contributing to the well-being of others by sharing the wisdom you have gained through your own journey.

Wisdom is not a static endpoint but an ongoing process of growth and refinement. It is the ability to navigate the complexities of life with grace, insight, love, and compassion. It is the understanding that the grass grows where you are nurtured, where you cultivate worthiness, build resilience, and seek enlightenment. It is the deep knowing that your journey, with all its twists and turns, has the potential to yield profound understanding and contribute to a more compassionate and interconnected world.

In conclusion, *The Grass Grows Where I Am* invites you on a transformative journey guided by these four essential pillars: Worthiness, Resilience, Enlightenment, and Wisdom. By cultivating a deep sense of your inherent value, developing the strength to navigate adversity, seeking knowledge and understanding, and integrating your experiences with reflection, you can cultivate a life that is not only meaningful and fulfilling but also a testament to the remarkable potential that resides within you. Embrace this journey, nurture the seeds of your own growth, and witness the flourishing of the extraordinary being that you truly are. For indeed, the grass grows where you are.

Connect with my team to grow your brand, vision, mission, charity, and ultimately yourself. Join us and become all you have wanted to be while being supported on your journey.

When you heal yourself, you heal the World, and it is in those pristine moments that your Grass Grows Greener and Life will flow easily and effortlessly all around you.

In Light and Love, Noah *Crane*
Author: *The Grass Is Greenest Where I Am*
Spotify Podcast Host: World Healing Tour
President Boca Raton Holistic Chamber 2024/2025
CEO World Healing Tour Events and Expo LLC

WORTHINESS

What "THE GRASS GROWS WHERE I AM" Means to Me

> *You carry growth, life, and possibility within you so wherever you are things can flourish. It's a reminder that your presence nurtures and brings value no matter the environment.*

Dr. Christine Abrahams

Connect with Dr. Christine:

Finding Worthiness in Label-Free Parenting

Christine Abrahams, EdD, NCC, LPC, LMHC, ACS

*How you love yourself is how you teach
your children to love themselves.*

—Rupi Kaur

I grew up in New York City, in a one-room, roach-infested apartment nestled in a neighborhood known as Chelsea. This wasn't the Chelsea of today, with its glittering art districts, upscale boutiques, and over 200 sophisticated art galleries. Back in the '60s and '70s, Chelsea was a raw, vibrant, and often challenging mosaic of life. It was a diverse place, characterized by its federal housing projects, the stoic walk-up brownstones, and an ethnic soup mixture of residents, each striving to carve out their existence in the urban jungle.

Our family was considered poor, a label that felt like a heavy cloak, because my parents perpetually struggled to meet our most basic needs: food, clothing, and healthcare. In all actuality, we weren't just poor; we were, by any measure, dirt poor, and this stark reality cast a long, stressful shadow over our family life.

The true, visceral understanding of our poverty didn't dawn on me through abstract concepts or the hushed whispers of adults. It arrived with a jolt, a single, indelible memory from my childhood. I must have been very young, but the clarity of that day remains etched in my mind as vividly as a photograph. My dad, a short-order cook, convinced me to embark on an "adventure"—a euphemism, I would later understand, for stealing food from the very restaurant where he worked, and where they trusted him. It is not every day that a child sees their father, a figure of strength and provision, running up the stairs, arms laden with stolen food, his voice strained with urgency as he shouted, "We have to go now!"

This was not a game; it was a desperate scramble for survival. He would also shoplift cans of tuna and even our clothing, a silent testament to his relentless struggle to make ends meet for our family. At the time, my child's mind processed it as a thrilling escapade, a secret mission with my dad.

It wasn't until much later, when the innocence of childhood had receded, that the crushing weight of that reality settled upon me: We needed to steal to survive. It was in this painful realization that the deeper, more unsettling truth emerged—both my mom and dad grappled with costly addictions—a revelation that began to chip away at the fragile scaffolding of my childhood sense of security and, subtly, my understanding of my own inherent worthiness. How could I be worthwhile, when this was the reality of my existence?

Yet, even amid the chaos and the gnawing anxieties of poverty and addiction, there existed within me, from a very young age, a profound and undeniable knowing. It was a truth that resonated deep within my heart and soul: I couldn't truly die. Not that my physical body was immortal, but "I"—that inner self, that pure awareness, that undeniable essence that was unequivocally *me*—could not perish. This was an intrinsic sense of worthiness, a fundamental understanding that my existence was not contingent on external circumstances, not defined by the squalor of my home or the struggles of my parents. It was a pristine, unblemished core, untouched by the external world. It was a feeling of being whole, complete, and eternally valuable, simply because I *was*.

As I grew older, however, this luminous "knowing" began to fade, much like the vibrant dye on my only pair of treasured blue jeans, slowly leaching away with each wash, each wear. The relentless pressures of my environment, the constant exposure to danger, the instability of a home shadowed by a drug-addicted father and a raging alcoholic mother, all started to erode this profound inner truth.

I began to believe and identify with the notion that I was merely a physical body, fragile and vulnerable, and that I certainly *could* die. This epiphany, this harsh reality of my own mortality and vulnerability, came to me countless times, each instance a stark reminder of the precariousness of my existence. Identifying with my body meant, to me, that I had to be hyper-aware of danger. It was an omnipresent force, lurking in every corner of our chaotic life.

This shift from an expansive inner knowing to a constricted focus on physical survival was a profound loss. For a significant period, I lost sight of the truth about who I truly was—not this vulnerable body, but something far more enduring and connected to a bigger, more universal message. The feeling of being inherently worthy of being unconditionally loved and safe was slowly suffocated by the fear of physical harm and the constant need for vigilance.

School as a Safe Haven

The external world, with its harsh realities and the painful lessons of my upbringing, began to define my internal landscape, replacing my innate sense of worthiness with a pervasive feeling of being unprotected and, at times, undeserving of peace. It was in this landscape of uncertainty that I discovered a profound sanctuary: school. It was a stark contrast to the tumultuous environment of my home. School was clean, a stark departure from the roach-infested apartment. It was structured, offering a predictable rhythm that my life desperately lacked. Crucially, it was drug-free, providing a haven from the pervasive addictions that shadowed my family. And perhaps most importantly, school engaged me creatively and academically, offering fertile ground for my mind to flourish. I didn't just attend school; I excelled at it, devouring knowledge and embracing the stability it offered. My teachers became more than just educators; they became healthy replacements for my mother, offering guidance, stability, and unconditional belief that I so desperately craved.

These extraordinary individuals saw something in me that was worth cultivating, something beyond the ragged clothes and the anxious eyes of a child from a struggling home. They saw potential, intelligence, and a spirit yearning for connection. Their belief was a powerful antidote to the subtle, corrosive messages of unworthiness that my home life inadvertently instilled.

My teachers didn't just teach subjects; they opened the world to me, validating my existence and reinforcing a true understanding that I was, indeed, worthy of their time, their effort, and their profound generosity. I remember my fifth-grade teacher, a woman whose quiet strength left an indelible mark on my soul. Upon my graduation from her class, she gave me a copy of *Siddhartha*. This was a remarkably sophisticated book for a fifth grader, a philosophical novel exploring self-discovery and enlightenment. Of course, at that tender age, I didn't understand a word of it. The complex themes of spiritual awakening and the search for truth were far beyond my grasp. Yet, I read it diligently, not for understanding, but because *she* had given it to me. The act of receiving such a profound gift from her felt like an immense honor, a testament to her belief in my intellectual capacity and my inherent worthiness of such a deep literary experience.

As an adult, I have reread *Siddhartha* countless times, each reading revealing new layers of profound wisdom. I often wonder why she chose that book for me, a child navigating the harsh realities of Chelsea. Perhaps she intuitively sensed the seeker within me, the child who had once known an undeniable truth about not being able to die and saw that the seed of that knowing was still there, waiting to be nurtured. Her gift was a silent affirmation of my potential, a beacon of light in a world that often felt dark.

Yoga

Another pivotal moment came in middle school when a teacher, recognizing a spark within me, asked if she could take me to an Integral Yoga class in Greenwich Village. In those days, the bureaucratic layers of parental permission slips were less prevalent, so she simply suggested I ask my mother. My drunken mom, whose mind was often clouded by alcohol and suspicion, immediately spiraled into a paranoid fantasy. Not knowing anything about yoga, she envisioned this as some nefarious scheme to sell me into white slavery. The absurdity of it was lost on her in her inebriated state.

After much pleading and reassurance from my teacher, my

mother finally relented, albeit reluctantly. And so, I went to that class with my teacher, stepping into a world that would forever alter the trajectory of my life. I have been practicing yoga ever since, a consistent anchor in my journey. This act of mentorship, this teacher's unwavering commitment to my well-being despite my mother's irrational fears, was a profound act of kindness. It reinforced, once again, that I was worthy of care, worthy of new experiences, and worthy of someone fighting for my growth. Yoga, in its essence, became a practice of reconnecting with that inner self, the one that had known its own immortality, and a way to cultivate a stable, unwavering sense of worthiness that transcended the external chaos.

Home as a Safe Haven

One fine day in seventh grade, a seemingly ordinary visit to a new friend's brownstone in Greenwich Village became a watershed moment, a profound epiphany that solidified my burgeoning sense of self-worth and catalyzed a radical shift in my life's direction. Her parents welcomed me with open arms, their warmth a stark contrast to the emotional chill of my own home. Their house was not just big; it was immaculately clean, radiating a palpable sense of warmth and safety. It was clear, with an almost aching clarity, that my friend's parents loved her very much, a love that manifested in the tangible comfort and security of their home. They offered me a big meal, and I ate greedily, savoring every bite, not just for the food itself, but for the unspoken nourishment of being cared for. When it was time for me to go home, they insisted on giving me cab fare, explaining that it was getting dark and they didn't want me to walk alone. Cab fare? The very concept struck me with an almost comical disbelief. They had enough money for cabs!

This simple gesture, a commonplace convenience for them, was a revelation to me. It shattered my limited worldview, revealing a reality where basic needs were not just met but where comfort and safety were readily available. It implied a different level of existence, one where people were *worthy* of such considerations. They hailed a cab for me, and as I settled into the back seat, alone in the quiet hum of the taxi, a series of vivid images began to unfold in my mind. I saw myself living that kind of peaceful life, a life of stability, warmth, and abundant love.

For the first time, this seemed not just like a distant fantasy but a tangible possibility. I thought of how much my teachers believed in me, how they had seen and nurtured a spark within me. I reflected on how, unlike the deeply dysfunctional families in my neighborhood, there truly were families that embodied functional love, families where care and respect were the norm, not the exception. And then, in the quiet solitude of that cab, I spoke aloud, my voice firm and resolute, echoing through the empty back seat: "I will never speak like my parents, act like my parents, or be like my parents, so help me God." This was more than a child's vow; it was a profound declaration of self-worth, a conscious severance from a lineage of dysfunction. It was a moment of radical self-acceptance, a decision to claim a different future, one where I was worthy of peace, stability, and a life defined by my own choices, not by the limitations of my past.

This turning point filled me with an unwavering resilience: the inner fortitude I needed to make my life meaningful. I consciously began to let go of what did not serve me—the fear, the limiting beliefs, the inherited patterns of unworthiness. It was the first conscious step on a long journey of shedding the labels and expectations that had been placed upon me, both by my circumstances and by my own developing narrative.

Religion

My parents, hailing from different faiths, created another source of confusion and pressure in my young life. My mother, a Catholic, forced me to choose a religion, demanding, "Pick one!" while my father was of Jewish faith. Neither religion spoke to my young heart. The sight of a bloodied man hanging from a cross terrified me, a stark and unsettling image. So, I chose Judaism, primarily because the rabbi, with a twinkle in his eye, promised weekly cake at Sunday school. Considering our usual scarcity of food, this was an irresistible offer. The services, mostly in Hebrew, were largely boring to my child's mind, but I found solace in the kindness and acceptance of the people there. They didn't judge; they simply welcomed.

As I matured, a deep curiosity about Jesus began to stir within me. I sought answers beyond the frightening image of the cross, and my quest led me to read *The Last Temptation of Christ*. While a work of fiction, this book offered a profound perspective, helping me to see Jesus, not as an untouchable deity, but as a person grappling with immense, human challenges. This portrayal piqued my interest in the New Testament, which I devoured with an insatiable hunger. Through these texts, I concluded that Jesus was truly ahead of his time, for he seemed to retain the very knowledge that I had suppressed or lost as a child: the profound truth that "The Father and I are One." This was the echo of my early knowing, the recognition of an inherent unity and worthiness that transcended individual form. As a result of this intellectual and spiritual awakening, I became a seeker, driven by an insatiable hunger for deeper truths.

Naturopathic Medicine

My personal path to enlightenment, believe it or not, began with a mundane medical condition. While working in financial services in New Jersey, I was suffering greatly from a persistent infection. My strong aversion to antibiotics led me to seek out a naturopathic doctor, hoping for an alternative solution. After I described my symptoms, he, to my dismay, offered me antibiotics. I firmly declined, and his response, delivered with a knowing gaze, became a profound metaphor for my spiritual journey: "Well, when you're in enough pain, you'll take the medicine." I left in a huff, feeling frustrated and misunderstood, and immediately called a friend to complain. She, with gentle wisdom, suggested I contact a local homeopathic doctor but cautioned me that he "might want to work on my spirit." I bristled at that notion, my ego resisting any perceived intrusion into my inner world, perhaps fearing what deeper unworthiness might be uncovered.

Yet, the pain of the infection, and the deeper pain of my unaddressed inner turmoil, was indeed becoming too much. So, despite my apprehension, I called him. I spoke to his secretary, making it unequivocally clear that I was only there to be seen for my infection and *not* my spirit. My resistance was palpable, a defensive shield against vulnerability. This remarkable man cured my infection in a mere two hours, a testament to his skill and a hint at the deeper forces at play.

More importantly, he began the long, transformative work on my spirit over several years. He became a pivotal guide, placing me firmly on the path to enlightenment. He introduced me to profound spiritual teachers and their teachings: Joel Goldsmith, the Christian Mystic, whose insights resonated deeply with my earlier understanding of "The Father and I are One," reinforcing the inherent divinity and worthiness of every soul. Then, Michael Brown, who created "The Presence Process," a methodology that helped me bridge the gap between intellectual understanding and embodied experience, allowing me to assimilate knowledge of my true self beyond mere concepts. And finally, James Swartz, my beloved Vedanta teacher, who taught me about the "self" and the ultimate, liberating truth that we are all already enlightened, already whole, already complete, and already inherently worthy.

Even though I was deeply immersed in this journey, and intellectually I understood the profound knowledge that I had lost as a child—the truth of my nonphysical, eternal nature—I still, at times, behaved unconsciously. The assimilation of this knowledge of my true self, this deep understanding of my inherent worthiness, was a gradual process, not an instantaneous revelation. The combination of Vedanta, which provided the foundational knowledge and which I have been studying for years, along with Transcendental Meditation, which offered the direct, experiential realization of myself, created a powerful synergy. This dual approach of intellectual understanding and direct experience motivated me to dedicate my life to helping others find themselves, to rediscover their own inherent worth.

Helping Others to Reclaim Their Self-Worth

While working as a counseling supervisor in education, I had the profound privilege of meeting with some of the most hardened kids, those who carried the heaviest burdens of pain and who often manifested as the school's biggest discipline problems. These children, often labeled as "troublemakers" or "bad kids," were struggling with deep-seated feelings of unworthiness, a sense that they were fundamentally flawed or undeserving of love and success.

In our counseling sessions, I would pull out a simple pencil, holding it up for them to see. "Imagine that this is you," I would begin, "pure awareness, pure love." I would emphasize that this pristine pencil represented their true, untainted self, a core of inherent worthiness that existed beneath all their external behaviors and the labels society had placed upon them. Then, I would ask them to tell me who they thought they were. They would begin to rattle off adjectives, both positive and negative, though mostly negative: "I'm stupid," "I'm angry," "I'm a failure," "I'm lazy," "I'm unlovable."

As they spoke, I would write each word on a separate Post-it note and meticulously stick each onto the pencil, one by one, until the entire pencil was completely covered. When they finally stopped, their eyes wide with a mix of surprise and recognition, I would ask, "So, where are you?" Almost invariably, they would answer, their voices tinged with a newfound understanding, "I'm completely covered." "Yes," I would affirm, "and your job in this lifetime is to remove all these Post-it notes and get back to who you truly are—love, light, and pure, ordinary awareness."

This simple, yet profound, analogy resonated deeply with them. They understood completely that the negative labels and self-perceptions were not their identity but rather temporary coverings obscuring their inherent brilliance and worthiness. I would also gently mention that once they left my office, they would likely forget this truth and go back to "sleep," falling back into old patterns and beliefs. But I would reassure them, "Don't worry, you will come back, and I will remind you."

This ongoing process of forgetting and remembering, of shedding layers and rediscovering the core, is the essence of reclaiming one's worthiness. Throughout my life, I have been incredibly lucky to encounter people who have served as profound portals to spiritual growth. These individuals, through their wisdom, kindness, and unwavering belief in me, provided crucial opportunities for transformation. I could have easily ignored these invitations, choosing instead to indulge in a pity party for myself, consumed by the narrative of my difficult past. But by grace, I always kept an open mind, and crucially, I was always hungry for the truth.

I truly believe that my true self, that core of pure awareness and inherent worthiness that I first recognized as a child, had a guiding hand in providing these opportunities, enabling me to see who I really am aware without labels. This profound personal journey, the shedding of my own "Post-it notes" and the rediscovery of my inherent worth, is precisely why I have created programs that heal, known as "Label-Free Parenting." These programs are not theoretical constructs; they are born from my lived experience, from the understanding that the labels we place on ourselves and our children, both externally and internally, are the primary barriers to realizing our true, unlimited potential and our innate worthiness.

My journey from a struggling child in Chelsea, burdened by the unspoken labels of poverty and dysfunction, to a person who understands the profound truth of inherent worth has equipped me to counsel parents effectively. I guide them to work toward achieving both long-term and short-term goals in parenting without labels. This approach is more than just avoiding negative words; it's about fundamentally shifting the paradigm of how we perceive and interact with our children, allowing their true, worthy selves to emerge unhindered.

It's just like the wise Naturopath once said to me so many years ago, "When the pain gets to be too much, you will take the medicine." For many parents, the pain of seeing their child struggle with self-esteem, anxiety, or behavioral issues often stems from the subtle, pervasive influence of labels—labels that limit, define, and ultimately erode a child's sense of worthiness. The "medicine" I offer is the Label-Free Parenting program. It provides practical strategies and a transformative framework to heal these dynamics.

There is always a solution, and when we work together, you will witness profound change within your child. This program, Label-Free Parenting, is designed to create tangible solutions for you and your child, empowering you to parent in an authentic, informed, and deeply connected way. It's about fostering an environment where your child can flourish, be confident in their own skin, secure in their own value, and fully aware of their inherent worthiness, unburdened by the weight of external expectations or limiting definitions.

Reflections for You

- When do you feel most confident and worthy as a parent, and what contributes to that feeling?

- How did your own parents or caregivers communicate messages (spoken or unspoken) about worth and love?

- In what ways do you measure your worth as a parent—by your child's behavior, achievements, or happiness?

- When you're hard on yourself as a parent, what fear or belief might be underneath that self-criticism?

- What would it look like to give yourself the same compassion and patience you offer your child?

- How can you model self-worth for your child through your words, boundaries, and self-care?

- When your child struggles, how can you remind yourself that their challenges don't define your worth as a parent?

- What is one small daily affirmation or ritual you could use to reconnect with your own inherent worth—separate from what you *do* or how your child *acts*?

Connect with Dr. Christine:

What "THE GRASS GROWS WHERE I AM" Means to Me

> *Choosing to live in a place of No Comparison, No Competition, and No Scarcity. I choose to live in my own love and light and share my unique gifts with the world.*

Noah Crane

Connect with Noah:

You Are Not Broken! You Are Enough! Believe in You!

Noah Crane

Be grateful for who you are, who you are becoming, and who you will be.

Knowing your self-worth and value, as I discovered, is crucial to getting what you want out of life. Self-worth begins with self-love. If you don't love yourself, how can you truly understand your own value?

Many believe they must earn self-worth by achieving, pleasing, or proving. Here's the truth: You are already worthy. Worthiness means knowing you are enough right now, not someday when you're thinner, wiser, richer, or more successful. When you stand in your worth, you stand tall, stop shrinking, stop apologizing, and start taking up space.

Embracing my worthiness opened doors for me and led to a fulfilling life. I share my story because it's easy in today's world to lose your sense of worthiness and settle for less than you deserve. Until worthiness became my pillar, my life was a scary roller coaster instead of a beautiful, loving dance. For years, I struggled with self-love, self-worth, and self-value. I was constantly running away from myself, quitting on myself, and rejecting myself. Inside, I felt invisible, numb, and alone.

Growing up, I was a sad child, and for years I even forgot how to smile. Years of abuse at the hands of my stepfather left me broken, helpless, and isolated. I wanted to hide from the world. Fear consumed me daily. I existed in a world of drama, fear, and gossip, letting my circumstances dictate my life, not realizing I had the power within me to change my life.

Above my bed, I had a poster by Albert Einstein that gave me hope. It read, "Great Spirits Have Always Encountered Violent Opposition from Mediocre Minds." When I was fourteen, these words inspired me to make a promise to myself: "I am going to have an amazing life!" But, as life went on, that promise became buried deep inside me. For years, I felt a faint flame inside, longing for something better, but I didn't know how to access it.

In my late twenties, I discovered Louise Hay's book *You Can Heal Your Life*. It gave me a new perspective. I realized I could heal my inner child and become whole. I started believing that I could create something different for my life starting now. I became a seeker of growth and transformation, reigniting that dim flame inside me. To change my life, I had to stand up for the little girl inside me who was hurting, lost, and confused. I realized, "I am worth it. I am not going to settle for less."

I took a deep look at myself and stopped my self-destructive behaviors and began with forgiveness—first for the adults who hurt me and took advantage of my innocence and eventually for myself. Forgiveness was very healing and freeing. I realized their actions were the result of their own pain, not a reflection of my worth. Through forgiving them, I found freedom from their hold on my life and compassion for both their struggles and my own. I understood that by continuing my self-work, I could shift, change, and re-create my life and future. That realization gave me strength and excitement for what lay ahead.

In my late twenties, I wanted to find my soulmate, settle down, and start a family. I remembered the promise I made at fourteen: to have an amazing life. Now, I could choose what I wanted and would not leave my future up to chance. I needed to step into my inner strength and do something I'd never done before. In the past, men usually chose me; I had to learn to choose for myself, stand in my power, and be intentional.

Knowing that finding my soulmate would take time and that dating could be disappointing, I decided to make it fun by turning it into a game—"The Elimination Game." Eliminating things in your life that don't serve you is a great gift you can give yourself. The Elimination Game, which I described in my book *The Grass Is Greenest Where I Am*, let me stay in control, so I never felt rejected. If someone wasn't the right fit, I considered it a blessing—they simply weren't for me. I was looking for that one special man to spend my life with, and all others had to be eliminated quickly. I was twenty-nine and felt like I had no time to waste. The Elimination Game had rules to keep me focused and empowered. Using it, I found my soulmate, Steven Crane, just three months later. We've been happily married for over twenty-nine years and have three wonderful adult children.

To step into my self-worth, I had to choose myself first and focus on what mattered most in a life partner. Choosing a loving and supportive partner has been a source of growth and happiness. Feeling safe, loved, and cherished daily is a gift I treasure.

I've been married to my best friend and soulmate for twenty-nine years, and every day I thank G♥d for him. We didn't date for years;

we got engaged a month after meeting and married six months later. People often ask, "Noah, how did you know he was the right man in such a short time?" I knew because I had a plan and left nothing to chance. I asked the right questions, listened for the right answers, met his family, and, most of all, knew I was worthy.

The inner work I did on myself helped me choose from a place of healing, not desperation, fear, or doubt. Settling was never an option. On the roller coaster of life, I'd rather be alone than next to the wrong person. Standing in my worthiness gave me power in the present moment and let me live life on my own terms. Loving myself has been the most important foundation for my success. This miracle story of finding my soulmate wouldn't have been possible if I hadn't discovered my own self-worth.

Healing is a gradual process, not an overnight success story. Healing your trauma, heart, soul, and past requires constant commitment to your personal evolution. It's a decision to never give up on yourself, knowing that every struggle comes with unforeseen gifts revealed only when you rise above your darkest moments. "The apple does not fall far from the tree" is true—our experiences shape us. If we didn't come from a stable, happy home, it's like learning a foreign language without guidance. Our traumas run deep, with many layers to unfold before finding our true self-worth. Knowing you deserve a better life than you had as a child is rooted in knowing you are worthy.

No matter what traumas you've experienced, know that you have the power to heal your life—one step at a time. Forgiving those who hurt you will give you the power to move forward. Understand that those who hurt you were themselves hurt and lacked the tools to do better. By giving grace and forgiveness, you free yourself from their actions and define your own present.

Compassion for yourself and grace for others are essential to healing and owning your worth. Holding on to anger, sadness, blame, and hate are obstacles to healing—they keep you stuck. Instead, choose to forgive, release, and let go to reclaim your voice and stand in your confidence. The more you let go of, the lighter and freer you will feel, and the higher you'll soar.

If you let your existence be shaped by the outside world, you'll never experience true inner peace. Your self-worth will be diluted by others' opinions instead of grounded in who you are. Self-worth is connected to your choices and the people you surround yourself with. Knowing your self-worth is essential to healing, brightening your life, and experiencing joy, peace, and happiness. When you know your worth, you won't tolerate people who don't value you. You'll stop pleasing others and set healthy boundaries to protect yourself, your energy, your family, and your time.

You Are Not Your Past
You Are Not Your Stories
You Are Not What You Own
You Are Not What You Do
You Are Not Your Problems
You Are the Light That Shines in the World,
Connect to Your Light and Shine.

Knowing my worth led me to my mission and purpose of helping others heal themselves. I know the struggle well, and we all need support and mentorship from those who have walked this path before us. Surround yourself with people who believe in you and see your potential, even when you can't see it yourself. Life should be a celebration of moments, even with its ups and downs. You are the captain of your ship and can navigate the waters of your life as smoothly as possible. Stop beating yourself up for past mistakes and be grateful every day—life is truly a gift.

The Grass Is Greenest Where I Am

Start using your words to empower your life and journey. Use them to build, not destroy. My mantra "The Grass Is Greenest Where I Am" reminds me that I am exactly where I need to be at every moment. Make sure you don't use words to beat yourself up or belittle yourself. Speak to yourself as you would to a best friend. Speak into what you want, not what you don't want. Listen to the words you say to yourself—they are the foundation of your worthiness and what you can achieve. Notice if you are pouring into your dreams or draining them. Use your words to water your life and harvest the fruits you desire. Communicate your needs and wants to G♥d and the universe—they are always listening. Your words create flow or resistance, so use them wisely.

*Your words create your world,
and your world is created by your words.*

Part of owning your self-worth is speaking power and possibility into your life daily. Use your words as a boomerang to attract blessings and what you desire. As you shift your life, you'll hold yourself to a higher standard, stop compromising to please others, and be unaffected by others' opinions because you'll know your own value. Notice what you put into the world with your words. Whether you say you can or say you can't, you're right. When you know your value, you'll feel comfortable saying "no" to things that don't align with you. You won't shrink in the presence of others, instead you will understand and recognize their humanity and struggles. You'll realize you always had the power within you, even when you doubted it. You'll no longer waste time proving yourself to anyone but you.

You'll choose people who love, respect, and believe in you, and never settle for mediocrity. You'll choose a partner who adores you because you deserve unconditional love—a deep soul connection with your best friend and partner. You'll know the grass truly grows where you are and accept abundance, knowing you deserve all the miracles and gifts the world offers. The journey is meaningful, though not always easy. Dig deep to find all the pieces of yourself so you can live feeling whole, worthy, and deserving of a happy, joyful, and peaceful life.

Time is precious—being intentional now creates the life you desire. You deserve to feel like you've won in this life. With the right guidance and plan, you can become the person you most admire. Get clear on what you want, declare it, and take a new path to achieve it. What you do today shapes your tomorrow, so today is the perfect day to start. Release your fears, doubts, and past stories to step into your power. Become your own best friend and trust yourself completely.

Looking at the big picture of your goals and the long-term impact you desire helps you choose the right direction and eliminate what doesn't serve you. Don't let the noise of the world distract you from your dreams. Stay intentional and present. Avoid chasing pleasure to escape challenges—you'll give yourself a path toward real growth, passion, and purpose. Knowing you are worthy of an amazing life is the first step to creating it. You can have what you acknowledge and desire for yourself. Your journey is unique; never compare it to anyone else's. Your story will inspire others to know their own value and not feel insignificant or invisible. Your presence and voice matter, and your healing is a critical shift for all.

Heal Yourself, Heal the World

Heal Yourself, Heal the World is a commitment to working on yourself, finding your inner light daily, and never giving up on your hopes and dreams. Healing is not linear but a continuous process of expanding and healing your heart. Life is your opportunity to become anything you want to be. With an open mind, an open heart, positive role models, and G♥d's guidance, you cannot lose.

The 3G Effect

It's not easy to change how you think, what you say, and what you do, and this is why I created the 3G Effect—to help myself and others stay anchored in a positive mindset with a positive attitude daily. By investing in yourself—having a Grateful Heart, Being Grounded in Love and Compassion, and Being Guided By G♥d—you will stand taller, shine brighter, attract what you truly want, and live the life you deserve.

You can use the 3G Effect as a daily reset to focus on what really matters and draw it into your subconscious mind, heart, and soul. It's living your life in a positive space of possibility and transformation daily to pull what you truly desire toward you.

The 3G Effect is simple. Bring the 3G image to mind or look at the image each day as part of your daily practice. By connecting to its powerful energy, you are immersing yourself in love and light.

1. A Grateful Heart

The first G of the 3G Effect is to have a *grateful heart.* Learn to have a grateful heart no matter what you are going through. Gratitude has the energy of flow. Gratitude will help you get unstuck, freeing you to move toward your goals and dreams. Because gratitude is not stagnant, when you connect to gratitude, you are in a place of possibility, presence, potential, and flow.

When you have a *grateful heart,* you feel charged up. You are saying yes to yourself by not letting your current situation affect you or beat you down. You are able to let go of your negative emotions by connecting back to your *grateful heart.* Gratitude helps you find the silver lining in every situation. Gratitude also lets you accept things as they are right now. You stop fighting and resisting by surrendering to all that you are and all that you are not. Gratitude is like learning a new way of being. It has the ability to encompass every part of your life with its uplifting energy. Just like your breath flows in and out of you so easily, so can gratitude.

Gratitude is that river of love you get to swim in daily if you choose. The more you practice gratitude, the easier it will become. Learn to look around you each day and find things to be *grateful* for. The more *grateful* you are, the better you will feel, and the brighter you will shine. The more *grateful* you are, the more you will attract incredible experiences, people, and things into your life.

2. Grounded in Love and Compassion

The second G of the 3G Effect is to be *grounded in love and compassion*. Most of our suffering is optional. If you are emotionally hurt or are constantly triggered by others, it is a sign for you to do more inner work. Dive deeper into yourself by finding love and compassion for yourself now. Whatever you want, wants you. Whatever you desire, desires you. What's most often in your way is what will help you expand the most. You won't grow through the easy; you will grow through your challenges, obstacles, and lessons. That is why growing deep roots and a strong foundation of self-love is critical to your success.

By being *grounded*, you are growing strong, unshakable roots by learning to love yourself and believe in yourself first. You do that by nurturing your heart, soul, and spirit daily. It's meeting yourself exactly where you are with love and compassion—not letting others' judgments or your past define you but rather defining yourself.

When you are *grounded in love and compassion*, you are in a place of forgiveness, letting go, and acceptance. You stop judging, rejecting, and making yourself bad and wrong. You learn to love all of you rather than only some of you. You are healing your inner child and becoming more whole from the inside. Most of all, when you are *grounded in love and compassion*, you are connecting to a positive charge of high vibrational energy and attracting toward you what you want.

By finding self-love and self-compassion, you will also deepen the love energy of your heart and will want to share it more with others. That is the true magic behind your self-healing. The more love and compassion you give others, the more love and compassion you will receive. That is just how energy moves. The world is round, and energy moves in a circle, so whatever you put out will always return to you. Being *grounded in love and compassion* will keep your life in a receiving state of love, compassion and high vibration.

3. Guided by G♥d (Universe, Source, Higher Power, etc.)

The third G of the 3G Effect is to be *guided by G♥d*. G♥d reminds us all that we are never alone. G♥d has always spoken to me through the messengers that come my way. A messenger is anyone who crosses your path, who contributes to your life in a beneficial way, who teaches you something new, and who opens your mind to possibilities and approaches you may not have been aware of before. They are here to help make your journey easier by sharing their own life lessons and experiences with you.

You are a beautiful creation of G♥d. G♥d is always beside you, below you, above you, and inside you. Learn to listen to G♥d's guidance by turning off the noise of your mind and the outside world. Have faith in yourself and your journey. You are enough! The lessons, challenges, triggers, rejections, and obstacles are all here for you to overcome, transform, grow, and learn. Believers say, "G♥d does not give you more than you can handle," even though, at some moments, it may feel this way. The more you do your inner work, the more connected you will feel to G♥d.

G♥d wants to guide you daily on your journey. G♥d does that through signals, people, rejection, and elimination. Yes, when G♥d closes one door, G♥d will open new doors of endless opportunities. Your job is to be open-minded by having trust in the process and G♥d's timing and continuing to do your work on earth. That is why it's called a journey because it's about building character and patience over time. There may be occasions when you think you lost the match, but if you stay consistent in your mission and purpose here, you will win the tournament. With G♥d's guidance and love, you will flourish into the best version of yourself.

Find time daily to thank G♥d, to connect to G♥d, and to ask G♥d for support. When you are in a space of being grateful to G♥d, you draw more beautiful experiences to yourself. You remain in high vibration and live your most uplifted life. You'll be more open to G♥d's guidance by opening your heart. G♥d wants you to win, overcome, and believe in yourself. Feel G♥d's warm presence guiding your life and shining a light on you daily. Ask for guidance and support, and stay open to wisdom and messengers sent your way. Be a seeker, have coaches/mentors, and educate yourself on what matters most for your success.

ACTION STEPS

1. First thing upon waking, visualize or look at the 3G Effect image.

2. Connect to the first G.
   Have a grateful *heart*. Put your hand on your chest and inhale and exhale gratitude.

For example:

Inhale, exhale, and say: "I am *grateful* for my life."

Inhale, exhale, and say: "I am *grateful* for my breath."

Inhale, exhale, and say: "I am *grateful* for my loved ones."

3. Connect to the second G.

    Be *grounded in love and compassion.* Say three things you love about yourself.

    For example:

    "I love my smile."

    "I love my hair."

    "I love my heart."

4. Connect to the third G.

    Be *guided by* G♥d through prayer and gratitude. The more you speak and connect to G♥d, the clearer your path will become. Acknowledge G♥d's love and support. Here are some ways to thank G♥d daily:

    Thank G♥d every time you get home safe.

    Thank G♥d for your loved ones.

    Thank G♥d for divine guidance.

Repeat the 3G Effect elements before bed and as needed throughout your day. The 3G Effect focuses you on the present moment. It doesn't eliminate challenges but clarifies what matters: gratitude, love, compassion, connection, and a positive attitude. This tool helps you create a happy, joyful life with *floward* movement—never stuck.

The 3G image is so powerful that I created a 3G Effect jewelry line to remind those wearing it to connect to their heart with positive manifestation energy throughout the day.

No Comparison, No Competition, No Scarcity

Live authentically, without comparison, competition, or scarcity. Live in your own love and light, and share your unique gifts with the world. Plant your seeds, water them daily, and your grass will grow greener and stronger than ever before. Intentional actions aligned with your goals, purpose, and dreams are key.

"Together We Are Won" is another motto I live by. We are always learning and sharing truth to collectively grow ourselves and our communities. No one becomes who they are meant to be alone. That's why I created my organization, World Healing Tour, where heart-centered leaders collaborate and create meaningful and uplifting connections in a conscious and mindful space.

This book, *The Grass Grows Where I Am*, with its eighteen experts, is a testament to knowing my voice has rippled across the universe and, with G♥d's guidance, brought to me those who know their worth. The full circle moments I've experienced, working with holistic healers, have helped me grow as a business partner, friend, wife, and mother. I look forward to connecting with you on your journey as we move forward together. Namaste, my friends—forever grateful, grounded, and guided by G♥d.

Reflections for You

- How can you step into your inner strength and worthiness daily?
- What can you eliminate that is not bringing you peace and joy?
- Is the language you use daily creating obstacles or positive flow?
- What gifts have you uncovered through your struggles?

- How can you practice self-compassion each day?
- What are you grateful for now? Can you also be grateful for your challenges?
- How has connecting with a higher power shifted your life?

What "THE GRASS GROWS WHERE I AM" Means to Me

> A mindset — cultivating a life (and a space) that reflects your truest, holistically healthy self. It's a reminder that beauty, peace, and abundance are not 'out there'—they're within you.

Carrie Leskowitz

Connect with Carrie:

Cultivating Your Space, Affirming Your Worthiness

Carrie Leskowitz

Home is a metaphor for our soul.

Life has a curious way of leading us on unexpected journeys, often resembling a winding path filled with circles, detours, and dead ends. As a college student pursuing my degree in psychology, I found myself captivated by the intricacies of the human mind while simultaneously following my passion for fashion.

Balancing my academic pursuits with part-time work as a visual merchandiser, I soon transitioned into the role of fashion show coordinator and stylist. The allure of the fashion industry was intoxicating. I chased my dream that led me to producing dazzling fashion shows and styling for television and print. The excitement of traveling, collaborating with creative minds, and dressing models and clients in the latest trends made me feel alive.

However, life has a way of redirecting your path when you least expect it. As I found myself pregnant with my second child, the landscape of my career began to shift. Opportunities in fashion were migrating away from Philadelphia to New York, and I had to face the fact that that chapter of my life was about to close.

Interior Design

In this moment of uncertainty, I turned to another passion: interior design. The seeds for this new path were planted by my mother, a woman of innate creativity who had made a hobby out of helping friends decorate their homes. Together, we formed a design firm, merging our talents and visions. This collaboration brought a fresh sense of purpose and fulfillment to my life, allowing me to channel my creativity into a space that felt both nurturing and transformative.

Shifting Perspective

Despite the external successes I was experiencing, an internal struggle was brewing. I felt "stuck" in an area of my life that was out of my control, and my mental and physical health were waning. After seeing many doctors and doing much research, I came to understand the importance of integrative medicine and the connection between holistic health and wellbeing. What goes on in the mind, goes on in the body. In the face of these challenges, I decided to become a life coach. I recognized that while I had little control over my circumstances, I did possess the power to shift my perspective. I clung to my identity as a fixer, a problem solver, a healer.

This transformative healing journey felt life-changing, and as I began to embrace my newfound knowledge, I noticed a shift within myself. Like a mirror, I began to see a reflection between my inner self and my outer self, my environment and my relationships, each influencing the other. I felt a deep yearning to share my insights with a broader audience.

I was no longer just creating aesthetically pleasing environments but crafting spaces that resonated with my clients' authentic selves, empowering them to express their identities fully. My design and coaching work, hand in hand, transformed my clients' spaces, with the goal being to create environments that improve overall well-being—body, mind, and spirit. I understood that our homes hold the potential to facilitate healing on a deeper level and had the language to guide clients through a holistic transformation.

Each design choice reflects not only personal tastes but also the emotional landscapes of those who inhabited the space. This realization marked a pivotal moment in my enlightenment journey. I recognized that the healing process begins with self-awareness, which leads to resilience, and my holistic approach to living emphasized the interconnectedness of body, mind, spirit, and living space. The notion of "home" evolved into a metaphor for self. It encapsulated not just your physical dwelling, but also the inner space you cultivate within yourself.

Just as I was feeling called to continue down this exciting path and serve my clients in a more authentic way, I unexpectedly and shockingly (in the case of my mother) lost both of my parents in a fairly short period of time. I found myself in a very dark and unfamiliar place. The grief was palpable, and my health took another downward spiral.

The business of interior design felt too cumbersome. I was not in the right state of mind to serve others in that way, but I still wanted to serve in some way. But what? In an ah-ha moment, when I was at my lowest, I asked myself, "What can I do to remain creative?"

This desire culminated in the publication of my book, *Om for the Home*. It was born out of a longing to inspire creativity and illuminate how intimately our living spaces reflect our internal beliefs, values and vulnerabilities to a broader audience. Many people overlook the potential of their homes to foster overall well-being and sustainable joy. The writing of my book became a cathartic two-and-a-half-year journey.

It was fortuitous that I received a call from my client, Robert, during this time. He wanted me to help him redecorate his home. Robert's parents had also passed, and their belongings had found their way into Robert's foyer and living room, physically blocking the natural traffic patterns. I knew Robert needed some coaching around the meaning of their things and to find freedom from the emotional grip they had on him so he could move them and move forward, feeling free to decorate authentically in his next phase of life. I had the language and the experience to hold space for Robert as he did the deep dive needed to clear his emotional and physical blocks and move forward.

Self-Acceptance

My journey toward self-acceptance and inner peace became paramount as I delved into this holistic perspective. Through my own journey, I learned the importance of showing up for yourself in body, mind, spirit, and living space. I stepped out of the darkness and into the light and designed a new home for myself that encapsulated my essence. My home tells the story of who I am and what I value most. It made me a firm believer that the grass grows where I am. My home is a sanctuary that I cherish and expresses who I believe myself to be: the best, healed version of Carrie.

Seeking beauty has always been a guiding principle in my life. It serves as my beacon, reminding me of the joy and inspiration that surrounds us. In the words of American interior decorator Elsie de Wolfe, "I am going to make everything around me beautiful; that will be my life." This mantra resonates deeply within me, fueling my passion not only for creating beautiful spaces, but also for fostering an appreciation for the beauty that exists within and outside ourselves. As I reflect on my journey, I recognize that resilience is not merely the ability to bounce back from adversity; it is the courage to embrace change, to learn from your experiences, and to grow through the challenges you face.

Worthiness is the understanding that you deserve love, joy, inner peace, and fulfillment, regardless of the obstacles that life presents; how you show up for others must start in a space that is filled with moments when you show up for yourself first. Your home, the tangible assets at your fingertips, the color palette you choose, and the time you spend with family, friends, and self are the moments that define your "OM." We are all works in progress, continually evolving and expanding our understanding of ourselves and the world around us. My journey has taught me that self-discovery and resilience lead to a level of enlightenment and inner peace that I am continually pursuing. When we acknowledge our worth, we cultivate resilience, and when we embody resilience, we affirm our inherent value.

I invite you to reflect on your own journey. Embrace the twists and turns, the moments of darkness and light. Recognize the power of your living space as a reflection of your inner self and a catalyst for healing. As you navigate life's challenges, remember that your resilience is a testament to your worthiness. You have the capacity to create a life that resonates with authenticity, beauty, and joy.

Celebrate your journey and step toward enlightenment within your personal spaces in your home, for it is within these experiences that you discover your true self and the beauty that lies within you. The small changes and fluid motion of life has led to personal enlightenment, and as a life coach, keynote speaker, Feng Shui, and art consultant I invite you to connect with me to help guide you in becoming the most authentic version of yourself. Your hoMe® is a metaphor for who you truly are in a space where you can be your most authentic self, a place you want to come back to again and again. That creates sustainable joy. Many of my clients have asked me questions over the years, and from the pages of *OM for the hOMe*, we understand the holistic approach to Interior Design for your overall well-being: Body, Mind, and Spirit.

Q: How does your home heal you on a deeper level?

A: Your home acts as a metaphor for who you are, what you believe about the world around you and within yourself. Many modalities need to be in place to allow you to be your best self, your living space being just one. Have you ever walked into someone's home and felt something was "off" or that it was a little too messy or disorganized? Conversely, have you been in a home that is too perfect or trend driven, in which you saw no expressions of the inhabitant's personality? These are messages.

Holistic design, at its core, is the understanding that everything is connected. Holism is defined as serving the whole. Your home is a pillar of wellness, as important as your physical and emotional health because each is influenced by the other. There are messages you want to get to the root of.

Healing your home or healing yourself first becomes a case of chicken or egg because they are intimately tied together. You cannot have a well-designed home that supports a healthy lifestyle while your mind is full of negative thoughts or negative energy. You cannot have a clear, enlightened mind if your home feels chaotic or in disrepair. If your home is cluttered, it stands to reason that another area of your life or your thoughts is cluttered. If your home does not tell the story of who you are, maybe you don't know who you are and what you value beyond scratching the surface. Your home is part of your human experience. It is a mutualistic relationship where one area can help shine a light on another area that may need your attention.

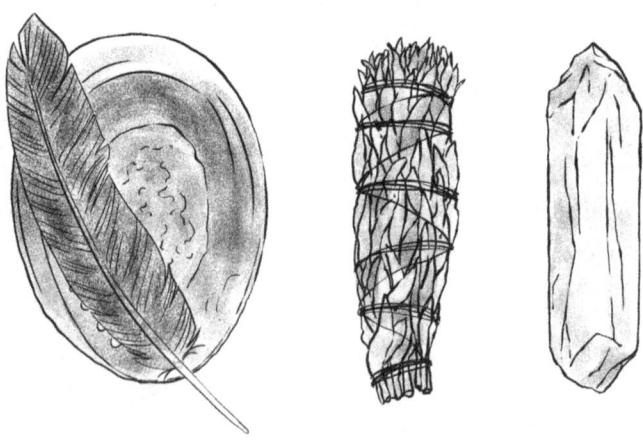

Q: What can you do holistically to improve the environment in your own spaces at your home?

A: Always ask yourself how a space makes you feel. Your home holds energy. Energy connects you to your emotional brain. First things first, the space needs to be clean and uncluttered. Be mindful of toxins lurking (in cleaning products, furnishings, air fresheners, etc.) and reduce those as much as you can. To really get a fresh start in a space, I love incorporating a space-clearing ritual in the form of a sage cleansing. Good light, preferably natural light, is essential; balance and harmony among objects help move your eye around the room; and a connection to nature has all kinds of health benefits.

Engage all your senses. Display fresh flowers and curate cherished objects in a grouping that you see often. I always have a bowl of fresh fruit on the kitchen counter; it expresses life, abundance, and health. Your home must function for the way you live and ideally should connect to who you are authentically. For your home to do that, you need to have done the "inner" work, so you master aligning your environment with your authentic self. That reinforces how good you will feel in your space.

Q: How can you train your own eyes to find beauty and think like an artist?

A: Everyone looks but not everyone sees. You can cultivate the habit of looking at things in a new way by being curious. Pay attention to the intricate markings of bark on a tree, the arrangement of books on a shelf, noticing when you feel moved during a concert, or the rush of adrenaline when something excites you. Be open to newness, explore new things, go to new places. Just changing your routine will allow your brain to see things in a new way. When you like what you see, it activates your pleasure center, and you get a shot of dopamine as a reward.

So, circling back, notice how you feel. Let's expand on that and provide some practical steps to train your own eye to find beauty and start to think like an artist:

1. Conscious Observation: Beyond Looking, Truly Seeing

- Slow Down: Our fast-paced lives often prevent us from truly appreciating our surroundings. Make a conscious effort to slow down and savor the moment. Take a moment to just look. Be present.

- Details Matter: Focus on the small things that often go unnoticed, like the way sunlight reflects off a puddle, the delicate veins of a leaf, and the subtle shifts in color in a sunset. These details are the building blocks of beauty.

2. Cultivating Curiosity and Exploration

- Explore Different Perspectives: Physically move around objects to see them from different angles. Crouch down, look up, get closer, step back.

- Embrace New Experiences: As I mentioned, venturing outside your routine is crucial. Visit museums, art galleries, botanical gardens, and different neighborhoods. Expose yourself to diverse visual stimuli.

- Travel (Even Locally): Even in your own town, you can be a tourist. Look for hidden gems, explore unfamiliar streets, and visit local markets.

3. Developing a Visual Vocabulary

- Study Art and Photography: Learn about composition, color theory, perspective, and lighting. Analyze the works of artists and photographers you admire.

- Sketch and Photograph: Carry a sketchbook or take a photograph. Capture anything that catches your eye. This helps you develop your visual memory and refine your sense of composition.

- Create Mood Boards: Collect images, textures, and colors that resonate with you. This helps you define your aesthetic preferences and develop a visual vocabulary.

4. Connecting with Your Emotions and Sensations

- Emotional Response: Pay attention to how different sights, sounds, and textures make you feel. Do they evoke joy, sadness, peace, or excitement?

- Journaling: Write down your observations and feelings. This helps you process your experiences and develop a deeper understanding of your own aesthetic preferences.

- Mindfulness: Practice mindfulness techniques to cultivate a sense of presence and heightened awareness.

Q: How can I tap into my own authenticity that aligns with my home's design?

A: Self-awareness is the cornerstone of observation or, as I stated above, self-awareness is the catalyst for all transformation to occur. When you are aware of what you are thinking, doing, feeling, and imagining, you have the power of insight and clarity. That's empowering.

Responsibility—only you are in control of you: your thoughts, beliefs, emotions, home, health. It is incumbent upon you to know yourself deeply so you can act in accordance with what's best for you. How you react to the ever-changing landscape of the world around you and take personal accountability allows for deeper relationships, more positive experiences, and contentment.

Energy—energy is everywhere and everything is energy. We are more than physical matter. Our homes are more than physical matter. We and everything in our home impact one another vibrationally. There are those things that you see, and there are those things that you feel. Different states of being emit different frequencies of energy. The practice of Feng Shui is the best tool to harness and balance energy in your home. A mindfulness practice is the best tool to create balance within yourself.

Q: What are the C.O.R.E. pillars of wellness of the home?

A: Connectivity—the understanding that everything is interconnected. There is a synergy between the body, mind, spirit, and living space. We must take responsibility to observe what feeds our soul, what raises our energy or drains our energy for a growth mindset and inner peace. Here's a deeper look into the principles and practices of holistic interior design:

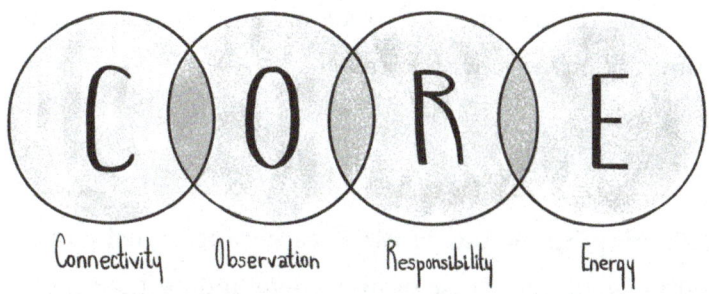

Core Principles

- **Well-Being as the Foundation:** The primary goal is to enhance the physical, mental, and emotional health of the occupants. This involves considering factors like air quality, natural light, ergonomics, and stress reduction.

- **Connection to Nature (Biophilia):** Integrating natural elements is crucial. This includes incorporating plants, natural materials like wood and stone, and maximizing access to natural light. Biophilic design principles aim to reconnect you with the natural world, promoting a sense of calm and vitality.

- **Harmony and Balance:** Holistic design seeks to create harmonious spaces that promote a sense of equilibrium. This involves considering the flow of energy within space, as well as the balance of colors, textures, and forms.

- **Personalization and Intention:** Each space should reflect the unique needs and preferences of its occupants. This involves understanding their lifestyle, values, and aspirations and designing spaces that support their individual well-being.

- **Sustainability:** Holistic design embraces sustainable practices, prioritizing the use of eco-friendly materials, reducing waste, and minimizing environmental impact.

Key Practices

- **Optimizing Space and Flow:** Creating functional and intuitive layouts that promote ease of movement and positive energy flow. This may involve decluttering, organizing, and strategically placing furniture.

- **Harnessing the Power of Light:** Maximizing natural light exposure and using artificial lighting to create a warm and inviting atmosphere. Consider the impact of different light temperatures on mood and well-being.

- **Selecting Natural and Sustainable Materials:** Prioritizing materials that are nontoxic, sustainable, and have a natural feeling. This includes options like solid wood, bamboo, cork, and natural fabrics.

- **Incorporating Nature:** Bringing the outdoors inside the home using indoor plants, natural textures, and views of nature. Consider vertical gardens, water features, and natural soundscapes.

- **Color and Texture:** Utilizing color psychology to create desired moods and emotions. Earth tones, blues, and greens are often favored for their calming and grounding effects. Textures are also very important, adding depth and natural feelings to space.

- **Creating Sensory Experiences:** Engaging all the senses using aromatherapy, chromatherapy, soothing sounds, and tactile materials.

- **Mindful Design:** This is the overarching theme, being mindful of every choice made in the design process and how those choices will affect the people that occupy the space. By embracing a holistic approach, interior design can become a powerful tool for enhancing well-being and creating spaces that truly nourish the soul.

My clients consult with me on Zoom to discuss their goals to elevate their vision, mission, brand, business, or clarity.

Reflections for You

- Is your home clean, organized and in good repair?

- Are there things you can say no to in order to feel freer, to maintain a state of inner peace?

- Connect to your body. Learn to listen to and trust how you are feeling. Your mind may lie to you, but your body never will.

- Do you engage in more activities (or with people) that light you up or dim your light?

- Have you thought about bringing nature indoors in the form of art, plants, sustainable furniture, organic forms?

- Everything is energy. Be mindful of the energy that is held in your home both through the objects brought in and the people occupying the space.

Connect with Carrie:

RESILIENCE

What "THE GRASS GROWS WHERE I AM" Means to Me

> *I embody God's Spirit and the unshakable resilience, strength, and wisdom of generations of women within me—empowering me to root deeply, rise boldly, and flourish in every season of life, while lovingly encouraging others to rise and thrive where they are planted.*

Sonia Artwell

Connect with Sonia:

Women's Wisdom: Nurturing Resilience Through Mind, Body & Spirit

Sonia Artwell

My mama always said, "Loss leads to legacy."

My earliest memories are bathed in the warm, humid embrace of Jamaica, a place of vibrant colors, rhythmic sounds, and the indomitable spirit of my mother. She was, and remains, the first and most profound lesson in resilience I ever received. Her dreams for us, her children, were bigger than the small island could contain, and so, driven by an almost fierce love, she set her sights on the Cayman Islands—a beacon of opportunity across the turquoise expanse. I remember her hands, calloused from hard work yet always gentle as they smoothed my hair or held me close. Her eyes, though often tired, sparkled with unwavering hope. She spoke of a future where her children would not just survive but thrive, where doors would open that had remained stubbornly shut for her. This vision, this unyielding belief in a better tomorrow, was the invisible thread that guided our journey, a journey marked by footprints in the sand, both literal and metaphorical.

Then came the night that forever etched itself into the landscape of my memory, a night that tested the very core of that inherited resilience. I was just a child, young enough to be dependent yet old enough to grasp the terrifying reality unfolding around me. Our home, the humble sanctuary my father and mother had painstakingly created, was on fire. I woke to the acrid smell of smoke, the crackling roar of flames, and the oppressive heat that pressed in from all sides. Panic threatened to consume me, but something deeper, something instilled by my mother's unwavering strength, kicked in. My siblings, all four of them, ranging from four years old to ten years old, were asleep. My mother was out of town, a fact that intensified the terror but also galvanized me. Alice, a woman staying with us, was still stirring. I remember shaking her, my voice a desperate whisper against the rising inferno: "Alice, the house is on fire!" In that moment of sheer chaos, fueled by adrenaline and a primal instinct to protect, she reacted. She had just enough time to grab each of us, one by one, ushering us out of the burning house, safely into the night. We stood there, huddled together, watching our home turn into a skeletal silhouette against the orange glow, the only things that survived, the children. My mother's relief, when she finally returned and saw us safe, was palpable. It was a raw, profound emotion that transcended words, a testament to the deep caring of family and the wisdom gained from sacrifices that had always been her guiding light.

To Endure: Channeling Pain to Purpose

That night, I learned that even when everything is lost, the most precious things—life, family, love—can endure. After the fire, my mother decided we would all leave Jamaica and join my father in the Cayman Islands. When we finally arrived in the Cayman Islands, the reality was a stark contrast to the idyllic picture my young mind had painted. We were immigrants, starting from scratch, with little more than the clothes on our backs and my mother's boundless determination. The struggle to survive was real, visceral. There were days when food was scarce, and I recall, with a pang that still echoes, my mother's quiet sacrifice. She would go hungry, picking from each child's plate, ensuring we had enough, even if it meant her own stomach growled. She lived the sacrifice, embodying it with every selfless act, and somehow, miraculously, we grew up feeling whole, nurtured under the incandescent light and guidance of her love. Her wisdom, gained from these profound sacrifices, seeped into my very bones, shaping my understanding of what it meant to endure, to give, and to love fiercely.

As I got older, the lessons of resilience continued to unfold, often in unexpected and painful ways. After my divorce, which involved abuse in several ways, I was tested as a parent. I leaned into the lessons of strength and was able to endure and move on. I began dating after my divorce, and like many young women, I found myself wrapped up with a man who, on the surface, treated me like a queen. He showered me with affection, compliments, and grand gestures, creating an illusion of perfect love. Yet, beneath the polished veneer, he was lying to my face, his actions betraying every sweet word. The realization was a slow, agonizing burn, a betrayal that cut deep. We had no children, no shared obligations beyond our emotional entanglement, and in that clarity, I knew what I had to do. Putting my integrity first, I made the excruciating decision to leave him. It felt like tearing a part of myself away, like I had to break my own heart by saying goodbye to someone I had loved, despite the deceit. I felt abandoned by him, but in that abandonment, I found fierce self-reliance. I made a vow to myself that I would never again betray myself just to be loved. It's a struggle many women face—the difficult choice between staying in a painful, toxic relationship or choosing to walk away and reclaim their power.

During this tumultuous period, something remarkable happened. I had already opened my second company, pouring my energy and passion into building something of my own. And as I navigated the emotional wreckage of that relationship, my business began to flourish. It was a powerful testament to channeling pain into purpose, to prove to myself that my worth was not defined by another's actions. I was not looking for anyone; my focus was entirely on my work, on healing, and on rebuilding my sense of self. What I have learned through every twist and turn of this journey, from the ashes of our burning home to the ashes of a broken heart, is this profound truth:

Everything I think and say affects my entire being.

The Architect Within: Thoughts Design, Words Build, Resilience Makes It Unshakeable

Our minds, our very thoughts, are not passive observers of our lives; they are active architects of our health, our happiness, and our resilience. The constant chatter, the self-doubt, the worries—they don't just exist in a vacuum. They manifest physically, emotionally, and spiritually. This realization led me to embrace simple, yet transformative practices: mindfulness, meditation, daily affirmations, visualization, and the intentional management of chaos. I discovered that feeding the mind with positive, empowering thoughts is as crucial as feeding the body with nutritious food. It's about cultivating an inner landscape that supports growth, peace, and strength. It's about understanding that our health, in its most holistic sense, is not merely the absence of disease but a vibrant state of being that stems from nurturing our mind, body, and spirit in harmony. My mother, in her quiet strength and unwavering love, lived this truth long before I could articulate it. She didn't have the language of mindfulness or affirmations, but her actions embodied them. Her spirit, unbroken by hardship, was a beacon. And that's what I want to share with other women, especially midlife women who are often at a crossroads, juggling so much and sometimes losing themselves in the process.

I understand what it feels like to stand at a crossroads, having given so much of yourself to everyone else, holding it all together—often in silence and on your own—to feel like your body and life are betraying you. I'm here to remind you gently and truthfully that your worth is not defined by your struggles or your past. You are not broken; you don't need to be fixed. It's time to remember who you truly are because true healing and real success begin within you.

The "Work In"

This journey has also led to my calling to design retreats—immersive, soul-stirring experiences where women can truly embark on a "work in," not just a "work out." Imagine a Bahama-based sanctuary where the gentle rhythm of the ocean provides the backdrop for deep healing. These retreats are designed to use music, dance, and movement as powerful tools to heal trauma held in the body, mind, and spirit. It's about reconnecting with our innate wisdom, releasing what no longer serves us, and rediscovering the joy and freedom within. We'll engage in mindful movement sessions, guided meditations, and workshops focused on reframing our narratives. There will be communal meals, opportunities for quiet reflection, and empowering discussions, all designed to foster a profound sense of sisterhood and personal transformation.

The GLOW movement—*Great Lessons of Women*—is more

than just a movement. It's a radiant ecosystem … a living breathing community designed to ignite transformation from the inside out. At its heart, GLOW is about creating a ripple effect. Because when one woman rises, when one woman grows, that growth doesn't stop with her. It sparks something powerful in another woman, and then another … until whole communities, companies, and even cultures begin to rise together. The GLOW Business Collective hosts The GLOW Conference to empower women in business through shared resources, mentorship, funding initiatives, and collaboration opportunities with other GLOW businesswomen. It's a business conference, yes, but one rooted in the heart, where donated funds help women who have a dream, a vision, or an invention—but who lack the necessary resources—advance their expertise, grow their enterprises, and connect with others who share a vision of purpose-driven success.

Through GLOW Media, I envision filming and showcasing authentic stories of GLOW Women—their journeys, their vulnerabilities, lessons, and their triumphs—in formats like interviews, documentary-style segments, and morning show features. It's a space where we acknowledge that no one is perfect, but together we can always find a solution. The value of GLOW lies in its collective wisdom, its supportive network, and its commitment to empowering women to step into their full potential as entrepreneurs and business leaders, to lead by example, and to create their own definitions of success. Through GLOW, we cultivate resilience, amplify voices, and build bridges between business and well-being, spirit and strategy, leadership and love.

My life up till now has been a testament to the power of resilience, forged in fire and refined through heartache. It has taught me that the greatest work we can do is the work within. As I always say, "It's time to do a work in, not a workout."

This is my guide to creating success, not just in business, but in life—a success measured by inner peace, unwavering spirit, and the profound ability to rise, time and time again, like a phoenix, from ashes to radiance. I have come to believe that we are not merely temporary vessels of flesh and bone but three-part beings: a spirit, a mind, and a body. The real me, the eternal essence, is a spirit. This spirit resides within a physical body, which allows me to breathe and move in this world, and it is governed by a mind, the seat of my intellect, emotions, and choices. I've learned that, while the spirit can exist without the body and mind, the body and mind cannot survive without the spirit. To navigate this temporary earthly existence effectively, it is vitally important that we feed all three: our spirits, our minds, and our bodies.

Spiritual Enlightenment

My journey toward spiritual enlightenment began not in a moment of tranquility but during profound pain. Like so many, I have experienced my share of undesirable circumstances, betrayal, loss, and the kind of paralyzing emotional pain served up on a hefty platter by the notorious server called LIFE. Yet, through it all, a constant voice from my mother has echoed in my mind, a beacon of hope and a guide for my soul: "*God never gives us more than we can bear. Just pray to God,*" she would say. This wisdom became the foundation of my path, a constant reminder that seeking God first, above all things, is paramount to our individual journey on earth.

This isn't just a simple act of prayer; it is a profound "Work In," a deliberate and continuous turning inward to commune with the source of all being. It is the path to enlightenment, the shedding of illusion to become fully aware of one's true, divine nature.

Into the Garden: Surrender Empties the Bags; Grace Fills the Soul

Every morning, the very moment I become aware that I am awake, a wave of profound gratitude washes over me. The first words I utter with exuberance are: *"Thank you, God, for waking me up this morning. Thank you for putting me on your wake-up list."* This simple expression of gratitude is the first step in a conscious act of spiritual ascension. I turn off my alarm and, rather than immediately engaging in the world, I go within. I retreat to a special place of calm, peace, and reverence, a sacred garden that exists solely within me. This is where I go to meet with my God, my Creator, to connect my spirit to His spirit and to be fed by Him.

As I cross the threshold from the chaotic world of my mind into this inner garden, the heaviness, the dirt, the grime, and the scars of this world begin to vanish. They dissipate in the brilliant glow of His marvelous light. This garden is incredibly beautiful, a place where super colorful flowers bloom, and vibrant trees stand tall. A magnificent waterfall, symbolizing the unending flow of divine grace, cascades from a mountain at the far end. With me, I carry two large black construction garbage bags, one in each hand. In these bags, I have consciously placed all the burdens of my human existence: my fears, my doubts, my worries, my concerns, my relationships, my "situationships," my stressors, and everything that no longer serves me well. These bags are the physical manifestation of the mental and emotional baggage that obscures my true, enlightened self.

As I walk toward our meeting place, God's presence, His glory expressed in a brilliant luminescence of light, shines upon me. Encircling His throne, I can see a host of angels in their heavenly garments, gently saying, "Holy, holy, holy, Lord God, Almighty."

The brilliance of God's light is so powerful that my eyelids fail to stay open. With every step I take, moving closer to the spirit of God, the transformation begins. The two construction garbage bags begin to grow lighter, my feet feel weightless, and I begin to move in slow motion as if transcending the earthly plane. I feel my crooked spine aligning, the bulging discs in my cervical spine popping back into their created position. The excess adipose tissue and scars, the physical reminders of my earthly struggles, fall away from my body. My muscles tighten, my skeletal frame straightens to what it was on the day I was born, and my skin becomes wrinkle-free and smooth as a baby's. My hair grows long, thick, and beautiful; my teeth, my body, everything begins to heal. Every single cell in my body is restored just by being in the presence of His glorious spirit light.

This physical restoration is a powerful metaphor for the profound spiritual purification that takes place. It is a return to a state of innate purity and wholeness, a prerequisite for genuine enlightenment. When I finally reach our meeting place, just before His throne, I raise both hands, leaning back for momentum, and with all my might, I throw the two huge black garbage bags into His presence. As I do so, His voice echoes in my soul, *"Cast all of your cares upon me, because I care for you."* The moment they leave my hands, the bags instantly disappear as angels snatch them away. You see, no sickness, no disease, no fear, no doubt, no lack, and no pain can ever stand in His presence. It is a powerful act of surrender, the ultimate shedding of illusion and ego.

The leap of faith that I take by living an enlightened life has brought me profound wisdom. He then tells me to hop up into the palm of His gigantic right hand. He tells me to just rest and lay there for a moment in the stillness. In that sacred moment, He begins to speak to me, to provide answers, guidance and reassurance regarding the things that are important to me. The feeling of peace, wholeness, clarity, perfect health, abundance, beauty, and fearlessness that I experience defies human language. It is the pure state of an enlightened consciousness. Then HE says, *"Okay, it's time to go into the world today, my child."* Every day, I must take a leap of faith to step out of my spirit garden and into the new day. I accept that I will encounter both obstacles and displeasure from others, but I choose to face it with this newfound spiritual strength.

Emancipate the Mind—Your Thoughts Are the Keys, Choose Freedom

The mind can be a prison or a sanctuary; the choice is in the keys you hold. The keys are your thoughts. I believe thoughts are spirits and we have the free will to choose which ones to welcome into our mind and which to gently release. Each day, I consciously feed my mind. I engage in deep honest conversations with God, me, myself, and I, nurturing my inner dialogue. I embrace the practice of "I Am" affirmations, knowing that what follows those words shapes who I become. The attitude of gratitude is deeply rooted within me, and I express it daily through thankfulness and appreciation to God, the universe, and the people who enrich my life. This practice nourishes my mind and uplifts my mental state.

Through personal declarations, meditations, carefully chosen media, prayer, music, and reading God's Word, I nurture my mind to grow into the highest expression of myself. This expression is not defined by societal expectations, social media, or the opinions of others but by my spirit—the real me—connected to and guided by God's Holy Spirit. Transformation begins with the renewing of your mind. Every experience in life starts as a single thought. The thoughts you dwell on take root, shaping the words, and those words in time become the world you live in. As Scripture teaches, "Life and death are in the power of the tongue. . . ." Your mouth is a garden, and every word is a seed. Each one carries the power to produce after its kind. Plant orange seeds and you will harvest oranges; plant apple seeds, and apples will come.

So, I ask you, what are you planting and growing with your mouth? Are you speaking words of life into your situations, into your children, into your finances, into your body? Or are you sowing seeds of death with careless words? Guard both your mind (thoughts) and your mouth. Refuse to let any thought take root, or any word to escape your lips, that does not align with your goals, desires, or your God-given vision. If you do not want it to manifest in your life, do not speak it. Ask yourself, are you consciously nourishing your mind each day with empowering thoughts that unlock your true potential? Or do you find yourself trapped, a captive within the prison walls of fear, doubt, or negativity that you have built?

Your mind is the key to your freedom. Nurture it, and you rise; neglect it, and you remain captive. As the reggae music icon *Bob Marley* sang in his Redemption Song, *"Emancipate yourself from mental slavery, none but our self can free our mind."* Choose to break free and live boldly.

Loving the Lumps: Compassion for a Changing Body Rewrites the Story of Health

The body is the sacred home of the mind and spirit. I always considered myself healthy in my mind with no medical conditions, no treatments needed. Yet, unexpectedly, I contracted a stomach bacterium that ravaged my gastrointestinal system. The pain, the chronic fatigue, the foggy mind, and the inability to absorb nutrients dragged me into a year-long battle of confusion and suffering in silence. I couldn't understand why my body, which I had always cared for with nourishing foods, was betraying me. Then came the weight gain, fast and unexpected. I gained twenty-five pounds in just a couple of months. My once familiar curves shifted dramatically; my clothes no longer fit, and my daughter's teasing words, *"Mom, you're just thicker than a Snickers,"* were a bittersweet reminder of the changes I faced. Having helped others improve their health and shed unwanted weight, I found myself asking: Why was this happening to me? Why now? The chronic fatigue was the hardest to bear, it drained me physically and emotionally. In my darkest moments, I pleaded, *"God, you created me; please heal me."* Traditional medicine offered no cure.

So, I took control of my healing journey. I studied everything I could get my hands on, from research papers to the leading experts on gut health. I became intentional and vigilant about every bite I took, every sip I drank, and every supplement I introduced to my body. Through nourishing myself with real, whole foods, pure water, and carefully chosen supplements, I was able to conquer that destructive bacteria. I had to learn to love my "lumpier lady lumps," to speak kindness and gratitude to my body for carrying me through so many years of life. The greatest revelation was that healing wasn't just physical, it was a profound "Work In." I had to dive deep into my spirit and mind to fully restore my body. Today, I'm filled with gratitude. Thank you, God. Now, I'm doing the "Work Out," rebuilding my strength, tone, and muscles with renewed purpose and joy.

Our bodies often manifest what the mind suppresses and the spirit carries in silence. Physical symptoms are not random. When your body is unwell, it's whispering the story of your inner imbalance . . . the emotions unhealed, the thoughts unguarded, the spirit unheard. Listen! When you pause to listen with compassion, your body becomes a messenger, a sacred signal calling you home to your true self.

Think it. Feel it. Say it. Live it.
I live by this mantra. You can make it your own.
—SONIA ARTWELL

Think it—I consciously choose the thoughts that shape my life.

Feel it—I let my heart truly believe it's already mine.

Say it—I speak life, power, and possibility into my dreams.

Live it—I walk boldly, moving and speaking as if it's already real.

The title of this book, *The Grass Grows Where I Am,* is screaming the same divine truth: "I am" is God, the grass grows where He is. "I am" (God) or your own divine source lives within you, within your spirit. So wherever you are, "I Am," the grass must grow. This is the ultimate truth of enlightenment; it is the realization of the divine spark within and the power that comes with living from that place of spiritual awareness.

GLOW for Growth

***As a holistic practitioner and wellness leader inside events and media production, I thrive as a holistic retreat facilitator.* I am called to speak, lead, and create impact for women creating simple practices that feed** *the mind, body, and spirit.* **I speak at**

corporate functions that link women's wisdom (the great lessons) to the concept of nurturing resilience. My programs, including GLOW, are a holistic approach (mind, body, spirit) to help you grow spiritually, mentally, emotionally, physically, financially, and socially. I look forward to discussing our collaboration and would love to connect. Our teams are seeking meaningful partnerships and collaborations with media outlets, corporate leaders, nonprofit organizations, businesses, and local individuals who would like to use our GLOW "Great Lessons of Women" approach inside wellness retreats. GLOW corporate team-building programs will add value inside your growing company where everyone thrives.

> *Imagine a team that trusts each other deeply, communicates openly, and returns to work energized and inspired. Imagine individuals walking away with a renewed sense of purpose, clarity, and confidence. That's what our retreats deliver. We create transformative, immersive retreat experiences where people disconnect from the noise, reconnect with themselves and each other, and leave with practical tools to move forward in life and work, with purpose and impact.*
>
> *Come GLOW with us.*

For companies, it's an investment in culture and performance. For individuals and couples who are ready for personal healing and life-changing solutions, it's a turning point. And for our partners and collaborators, it's a chance to be a part of lasting transformation. The only question is: Are you ready to grow the grass where you are and create the breakthrough that you will remember for the rest of your life? Work with us, we are waiting to work with you. God Bless.

Reflections for You

- When was the last time you truly felt like yourself—whole, seen, valued, and alive—and what layers of expectation or pain have you worn since then that dimmed your light?

- In what ways have you betrayed your own truth—silenced your voice, ignored your intuition, or abandoned your needs—just to be chosen, accepted, or loved by someone else? Where have you given away pieces of yourself to stay connected to others?

- What is the tone of your self-talk—is it nurturing or neglectful, loving or critical—and how would your life shift if you began speaking to yourself with the same compassion you give to those you love?

- What is your body trying to tell you through her whispers—her fatigue, her tension, her cravings, her restlessness—and what would change if you truly listened?

- Where in your life are you forcing instead of flowing—trying to hold together what your spirit has already released—and what peace might unfold if you simply let go?

- What daily rituals, boundaries, or sacred pauses help you return to your center—to the woman you are beneath the noise, the roles, and the responsibilities? If you could speak directly to the woman within you—the wise, resilient, radiant one—what would she thank you for, and what would she gently ask you to remember now?

Connect with Sonia:

What "THE GRASS GROWS WHERE I AM" Means to Me

> *If I love myself, care for myself, and nourish myself, no matter where I stand or what stage I am in life, I will be happy, healthy and content! I am the green grass!*

Leslie Carmen

Connect with Leslie:

Trigeminal Neuralgia: The Cost of Silence & the Resilient Fight for Life

Leslie Carmen

Hope isn't found in the absence of pain—it is born in the decision to believe there is something beyond it.

Life was good, with its usual ups and downs. Florida was warm, peaceful, and beautiful. My parents were still alive, doting on my daughter, Lee, who was, and still is, the reason I find purpose in my everyday life. There was a rhythm to it all, one that I deeply appreciated. Moments of gratitude filled my days, even if I didn't fully grasp the depth of what it means to simply have your health.

And then everything changed. It started with a phone call. "Mom, my tooth hurts," Lee said. It sounded minor, almost forgettable. A low-level emergency at most. Lee was in Lake Placid, New York, attending prep school on an ice hockey scholarship, and I was in South Florida. I called the school nurse. Then the dentist. I sent her a special homemade toothpaste. She tried Aleve. Nothing helped. The pain only escalated. Still, I clung to the idea that it was just a stubborn cavity or maybe a dental infection. But each day her discomfort grew more severe. Soon, unbearable.

I remember pacing my house, feeling helpless, wondering what on earth was going on with her. If it wasn't a cavity then what was it? The distance between us felt like an ocean. I was desperate to help her but stuck over a thousand miles away. Then came the second call. Lee was being rushed to the ER in the Adirondacks. The pain had reached a new level where she was now screaming. Shocks coursed through her teeth and face. Nothing soothed her. She was beside herself.

Trigeminal Neuralgia

Her father and I dropped everything and flew up to the Adirondack Medical Center. We arrived breathlessly, terrified, not knowing what to expect and just prayed someone had answers. And they did. Lee was diagnosed with a condition called trigeminal neuralgia. At first, I felt relieved. A diagnosis meant direction, a treatment, a cure for sure! But then I did what every parent does when the hospital quiets down and the mind starts to race: I Googled it. And everything changed again. *Trigeminal neuralgia* is also known as the *Suicide Disease*, labeled one of the most painful conditions known to humankind. My body froze and my heart pounded. My mind spun into overdrive. How could this happen? What did I do wrong? Was it something during my pregnancy? Did I miss something?

Would I lose my daughter? My best friend in the world? I looked over at Lee, lying drugged and sedated in a hospital bed. Her brave, athletic body, once unstoppable on the ice, was now barely able to hold a conversation. She was seventeen. This couldn't be her fate. This wouldn't be her fate. We brought her home and I decided I would turn over every stone and knock on every door. I didn't care what the research said, I was going to find a way to help her.

We had to take her out of school and as she lay in her bed back home, her future resting in God's hands, I began mine: a tireless search for healing. I had no clue where it would lead, but I knew one thing with absolute certainty. We were not giving up. Working during the day and surfing the internet at night became my new routine. In between, we visited neurologists, hoping and praying for answers. But the only advice we were given was to keep Lee on heavy-duty painkillers and seizure medications. They dulled the pain, yes, but they dulled everything else too. My bright, funny, full-of-life daughter became a shell of herself. A zombie.

I remember taking her to the mall one afternoon, thinking maybe a little outing would lift her spirits. We used to laugh and sing on those car rides, Lee and I, dancing in our seats to whatever was playing on the radio. But now, she sat slumped against the window, eyes closed, exhausted before we even arrived. We were at the Boca Center Mall for no more than twenty minutes before she turned to me and whispered, "Can we go home?" She was too tired. Too fogged up. Even the simplest joys were out of reach. Sleep became her only escape.

Fighting back tears and clinging tightly to my prayers, I kept searching. I wasn't going to stop. At work on my lunch break, I came across a website that mentioned a few patients with trigeminal neuralgia who had found some relief using laser therapy. Laser therapy? Bursting with hope, I called the LaserMed Center in Myrtle Beach, South Carolina, that very second. I connected with Nicole, who spoke to me for over an hour. She was warm, patient, and incredibly knowledgeable. She explained how their specific type of laser therapy had helped other patients, though there was very little mainstream information available. Still, something in her voice, something in my gut told me this was it. I had prayed for guidance and felt this was the answer. All the other treatment options came with massive side effects, and I couldn't bear the thought of putting Lee through more pharmaceutical trauma unless it was the very last resort.

Holistic Approach

I wanted to try the holistic route first. Deep down, I believed healing was still possible. I had grown up in Switzerland, where I attended a medical technical school. There, even many traditional doctors respected homeopathy, herbal remedies, and alternative healing. I'd been raised to think outside the box before resorting to aggressive interventions. Our minds were made up. We were going to South Carolina. I hung up the phone with Nicole on Thursday. By Sunday night, Lee and I were already sitting in our first consultation with Roger, the engineer who had developed the very laser they used at the clinic. I trusted that God had brought us here. But I'd be lying if I said there wasn't a quiet voice in my mind, whispering questions: Is this safe for her brain? Are we making the right decision? Still, I kept telling myself, trust.

Ten days into treatment, Lee was still in pain. At breakfast one morning, she looked at me with glassy eyes and said, *"What if it doesn't work?"* She could barely eat. Even biting into a bagel was too much. She stuck to scrambled eggs, soft and manageable. I looked at her and tried to keep my voice steady, even though my heart was aching. *"Pumpkin,"* I said gently, *"it's going to work. The laser is helping. Sometimes it just takes a little time."* I was repeating Roger's words, lacing them with motherly encouragement. I had to stay strong. I couldn't let her see my doubts, my fear. If I lost my composure, she'd have nothing left to lean on.

So, we continued. And then, just a few days before the end of the treatment cycle, something shifted. Lee woke up, rubbed her eyes, and said, "*I feel better.*" I blinked. "*What do I mean? I feel . . . different. The pain is less.*" I watched, barely breathing, as she picked up a bagel, her first in over three months, and took a bite. No flinching. No tears. Just chewing. Swallowing. Smiling. Thank you, God. The words repeated in my mind again like a heartbeat. Thank you, thank you, thank you. Every cell in my body rejoiced.

The months of tension, fear, and uncertainty suddenly lifted, and I felt it, relief so deep, it made me cry. Silently, tears rolled down my face. I didn't want to alarm her. I just smiled through it all, grateful beyond words. Lee tapered off all her medications shortly after that. And our twelve-hour car ride back home to Florida? It was filled with laughter. With music. With silly jokes and deep breaths. With hope. It was the kind of drive I'd been dreaming of since the day this nightmare began.

We were home safely. Lee was tucked into bed, sleeping soundly. And I was sitting at my computer, absolutely buzzing with a new purpose. I felt electric, joyful, grateful, and alive. My daughter was healing. And now, all I could think about was how many other families were still in the darkness, just as we had been. Over 150,000 people in the United States are diagnosed each year with trigeminal neuralgia, many of them isolated in their agony. Most have been told there's no hope, no real treatment—just a lifetime of pain, masked with heavy drugs until the despair becomes too much. Far too many consider suicide the only escape from this invisible monster. But we found light. We had found a way out. And I was ready to shout it from the rooftops. "The first thing I'll do," I thought, "is share our story on the Facebook TN support groups. They're going to be thrilled to know there's real hope out there."

Sharing Our Success Story

Oh, how wrong I was. Within two minutes of posting Lee's story, sharing her pain, her diagnosis, and the miracle we had just experienced, I was bombarded with angry comments. "Don't post false hope!" "Get off this site!" "This group is only for people suffering with TN!" I couldn't believe what I was reading. My hands trembled as I replied, "I'm a mother whose daughter had TN. She is now healing. I promise I'm just here to help. I don't want anything in return." But more slander came. Accusations. Mockery. And then, the admin blocked me. I sat there in shock. Total disbelief. "Wait . . . what just happened?"

Still determined, I found another TN support group. This time, I softened the tone of my message. I was gentler, more cautious, less enthusiastic, more subtle, as if I had to apologize for being happy. Blocked again. This time it hurt deeper. I felt gutted. What on earth was going on? Wasn't this good news? Wasn't *hope* what people in pain needed most? I didn't understand it. But I knew one thing for sure: I wasn't giving up. If I can save just one person, it will all be worth it.

If social media didn't want my story, maybe Wikipedia would. I remembered the trigeminal neuralgia page I had come across in my early research. It had a "Notable Cases" section, surely this was the right place to share what we had lived through. I decided to link to my then-husband's Wikipedia page, Phil Carmen, a respected musician and producer, hoping the name recognition might help someone, anyone, pause and read the story. I crafted our post with pride. This wasn't fiction. This was our life. Finally, I thought. A place where the truth can live.

Each night, I sat at my computer like a woman on a mission, scanning the internet, searching for platforms, communities, anything, anywhere that would allow me to share the possibility of healing. I thought, "Let me check the Wikipedia page again just to make sure it's still there." My post was gone. Deleted. I felt my stomach drop.

Frustrated but not yet defeated, I found my way into the back end of Phil's page. There it was, a note from a Wikipedia admin: The story had been removed. No explanation. I added it back. I wrote that this was our truth, our experience, and it deserved to be told. Again, it was deleted, this time with a comment: "Requires third-party verification." Third-party verification? I wrote back. "We have medical documentation. Doctor's notes. Progress reports. Whatever you need, please just tell us what to provide." Silence. Cut off. And that's when it hit me. This is so much bigger than I realized.

Our every word, our every action, our every attempt to share truth, it was all being watched. Controlled. And if it didn't serve a particular agenda, it was silenced. Not questioned. Not debated. Deleted. I sat in my chair and felt the chill of reality crawl up my spine. This wasn't about one girl's healing anymore. This was about a system. One built on silence. On sickness. On suffering. And I was now, whether I was ready or not, stepping into a war I never expected. A war where healing threatened the status quo. Where hope was dangerous. Where truth was a liability.

I had been a mother fighting for her daughter. Now, I was a woman standing up to a machine. And I wasn't backing down. So, if I couldn't talk about it . . . I would have to prove it. With the unwavering support of my parents and my sister, I was blessed to receive the funding to open my own clinic in Boca Raton. I poured my soul into it, not just the resources, not just the energy, but the vision. A fire had lit inside me, and nothing was going to put it out.

Carmen Care

After immersing myself in intensive education, I earned multiple certifications, completed licensing, and found a compassionate medical director to work under. **Carmen Care** officially opened its doors on May 9, 2013. At first, I focused on what I knew laser therapy could already do, relieve chronic pain. Knees, backs, shoulders, arthritis, fibromyalgia. And slowly, the word began to spread. People were walking in with pain and walking out with hope.

Occasionally, I was given the opportunity to treat someone with trigeminal neuralgia. And each time, I saw flickers of the same transformation I'd witnessed in my daughter. A spark. A shift. A moment of light where there had only been darkness. But I couldn't stop there. While others closed their clinics for the night, I stayed up studying. While others went on vacation, I flew to workshops and medical conferences. I devoured books. Enrolled in courses. I traveled across the country. Interviewed experts. Obsessed over case studies.

My relentless curiosity, my mother's intuition, and my Swiss derived education with commitment to precision drove me toward something deeper. That's when the real breakthroughs began. Over time, I discovered that true healing wasn't just about the physical pain. It was never just the joint, the nerve, the muscle. Chronic illness, especially those that had "no cure," always had layers. Invisible ones. Underneath every diagnosis, I kept finding the same three culprits, repeatedly: Trauma. Toxins. Thoughts. Not always in obvious ways. Sometimes it was emotional trauma from decades earlier. Sometimes it was mold hidden in the walls of a childhood home. Sometimes it was a deep-rooted belief that they didn't deserve to heal. And that's how my signature protocol was born.

T3 Paradigm

I called it the T3 Paradigm, a revolutionary healing framework that treats the trauma held in the cells, the toxins stored in the body, and the thoughts imprinted on the mind. It became the foundation of everything we do at Carmen Care. Eventually, I designed the 21-Day Program, a transformative healing experience for those suffering from complex, chronic, or "untreatable" conditions. For twenty-one consecutive days, we treat our clients twice a day, layering powerful, noninvasive modalities to activate every level of the healing process. It's not a spa. It's not a pill. It's not a generic protocol. It's a healing revolution.

Clients fly in from around the world to participate in the program. Each journey is uniquely designed, but all include elements like:

- **Laser Therapy:** To release trauma stored at the cellular level and reduce pain without pharmaceuticals

- **StemWave (Acoustic Shockwave Therapy):** To stimulate regeneration and enhance circulation

- **Laser Energetic Detoxification:** To target specific toxins—heavy metals, mold, plastics, glyphosate, and more

- **Red Light and Icoone Therapy:** To support lymphatic drainage, boost mitochondrial function, and help the body clear what's no longer serving it

- **Emotional Healing:** To calm the nervous system and release unresolved emotional patterns

- **Muscle Testing with Resonish Training:** So, clients leave not only feeling better—but knowing what works for their body

- **Reiki and Energy Clearing:** To reconnect the body with its own innate wisdom and return to balance

It's an immersive, full spectrum reset, addressing body, mind, and spirit with care, precision, and deep, intuitive understanding. By the end of these three weeks, I often see people returning to themselves for the first time in years. Faces soften. Eyes brighten. Laughter returns. Some cry, not out of pain, but out of relief. They've been seen. Heard. And most importantly, they've been helped. This work is not just my career; it is my calling. But with such a result, I can't help but ask: Why was I silenced? What if I hadn't been? What if, rather than being deleted, mocked, blocked, I had been supported, heard, even amplified?

Remember that Wikipedia post? It was live for maybe a few hours, just long enough for one person to see it. A woman who found it, who read it, and it saved her life. I met her later, during my training at that same LaserMed Center clinic (which is now, unfortunately, closed). She approached me slowly, with tears in her eyes, and said: *"Thank you. You were the reason I came here. I saw your post on Wikipedia. I had lost all hope. But something about your words made me pause. And that pause gave me one more chance."* She got help. She got better. She got her life back. And then, like smoke in the wind, my post vanished. She searched for it. It was gone. She was shocked. Confused. I was furious.

And now, I am haunted by one relentless question: How many precious lives might still be here if my words had been allowed to reach them? How many sons and daughters, mothers and fathers, could have found a reason to stay if my story—our story—had been seen? How many souls stood on the edge, waiting for a single glimmer of hope, only to find the crushing weight of silence instead?

How many suicides weren't just a tragic end but the final act in a hidden crime? Because every post deleted, every voice silenced, every truth buried aren't harmless acts of moderation. They are quiet acts of violence against hope itself. When stories of healing are banned, when testimonies of light are smothered, it isn't just censorship. It's the complicity in the darkness that drives people to the brink.

So no, I will not apologize for my urgency. I will not quiet my voice to make others comfortable. Because silence doesn't just steal words, it steals lives. If one post, one message, one brave story can save even a single life, then I will keep writing. I will keep shouting into the void until every echo finds a heart to hold onto.

Understanding Trigeminal Neuralgia: Root Causes, Real Hope

At my holistic clinic in Boca Raton, Florida, *Carmen Care*, we've seen firsthand that *trigeminal neuralgia (TN)* doesn't have just one cause—and that's exactly why it's so often misunderstood and misdiagnosed. For some of our patients, the onset of TN followed a traumatic *car accident* and resulted in *severe whiplash*, where the cervical spine and cranial nerves were jarred and misaligned. Others developed symptoms after facelift *surgery*, where delicate facial nerves were inadvertently agitated. Some patients have been so desperate for relief that they've had multiple extractions and in heartbreaking cases, even pulled their own teeth, not realizing the pain was coming from inflamed or infected nerves, not their teeth. And then there are those who arrive with no obvious cause. But when we test deeper, we often uncover hidden culprits:

- Herpes Zoster Virus (shingles)

- Epstein-Barr Virus (EBV)
- Spirochetes

Parasites and Environmental Toxins

These infections and toxins can inflame the nervous system, particularly the trigeminal nerve, leading to the signature shocks, stabbing pain, and facial hypersensitivity that define TN. Understanding TN is the key that unlocks the truth to healing. TN, also known as "tic douloureux," is a chronic pain condition that causes sudden, severe, shocklike facial pain. It affects the trigeminal nerve, also known as the fifth cranial nerve, which is responsible for sensation in the face. The trigeminal nerve is one of the twelve cranial nerves that originate in the brain. It has three main branches that provide sensation to different parts of the face:

- Ophthalmic (V1): Controls sensation in the eye, forehead, and nose.
- Maxillary (V2): Controls sensation in the upper teeth, gums, lips, cheek, and lower eyelid.
- Mandibular (V3): Controls sensation in the lower teeth, gums, and lips.

These pain attacks usually last from a few seconds to a couple of minutes but can occur repeatedly, sometimes hundreds of times a day. While the pain is typically unilateral (affecting only one side of the face), in rare cases, it can affect both sides, though usually not at the same time. Between attacks, some people may experience a dull ache, throbbing, or burning sensation. The pain rarely occurs during sleep. Pain attacks in TN can be triggered by even light touch or common daily activities, including:

- Touching the face (e.g., shaving, washing, applying makeup)
- Brushing teeth
- Chewing, eating, or drinking (especially hot or cold foods/drinks)
- Talking or smiling
- Blowing the nose
- A light breeze or air conditioning
- Head movements or vibrations (like riding in a car)

The most common cause of TN is compression of the trigeminal nerve by a blood vessel (usually an artery) at the base of the brain. Over time, the pulsing of the blood vessel can wear away the myelin sheath (protective covering) of the nerve, making it highly sensitive and causing abnormal pain signals. Other less common causes (sometimes called "secondary TN") include:

- Multiple sclerosis (MS): A condition that damages the myelin sheath
- Tumors: Pressing on the trigeminal nerve
- Arteriovenous malformation (AVM): An abnormal tangle of blood vessels
- Stroke or facial trauma: Injury to the nerve
- Post-surgical nerve damage: Sometimes following dental or facial surgery; in some cases, no specific cause can be identified, which is then referred to as idiopathic trigeminal neuralgia

Diagnosing TN is primarily based on a detailed description of your symptoms. Your doctor will ask about:

- The type and severity of pain
- The location of the pain
- What triggers the pain
- How often the attacks occur and how long they last

A neurological examination is typically performed, and an MRI (magnetic resonance imaging) scan of the brain is often recommended. The MRI helps:

- Rule out other conditions that might cause facial pain (like tumors or MS).
- Identify if a blood vessel is compressing the trigeminal nerve. Dental issues are often ruled out first, as tooth pain can sometimes mimic TN.

While there's no cure for TN, various conventional treatments can help manage the pain.

Medications

- Anticonvulsants: These are the first-line treatment. Medicines like carbamazepine (Tegretol) and oxcarbazepine (Trileptal) are effective in controlling nerve pain by slowing down electrical impulses. Other anticonvulsants include gabapentin, pregabalin, and lamotrigine.

- Muscle relaxants: Baclofen may be used, sometimes in combination with anticonvulsants.
- Botox injections: Can be an option for some patients.

However, in our clinic, we have witnessed many patients healing from TN with our 21-day protocol and have given hope to those who suffer from this debilitating condition. This is my story of *resilience*, a mother's fierce fight for her daughter's life, and a testament to the power of unwavering hope. It's a story born from profound pain but, ultimately, one of profound healing. It reminds all of us that, even when faced with systems that seek silence and suppress truth and healing, hope will always find a way to flourish. For me, the journey to help Lee taught me a powerful truth: The Grass Grows Where I Am. I will continue to cultivate that growth, ensuring that our story, and the hope it carries, reaches every soul yearning for light in the darkness. Please join me at my clinic and learn more about Carmen Care and how we can work together to create solutions that heal from the inside out, together.

Reflections for You

- What is the true cost of silence? When truth is suppressed, who suffers most? The messenger, the silenced, or the unseen lives that might have been changed?
- Where does responsibility begin and end? If sharing hope could save someone's life, do we have a moral obligation to keep speaking, even when the world doesn't want to listen?

- How do we measure courage in the face of censorship? Is courage found in shouting louder, or in quietly persisting until truth finds a way to be heard?

- What happens when hope becomes controversial? Why does society fear stories of healing, and what does that say about our relationship with truth?

- Can silence ever be innocent? When platforms delete messages meant to help others, is that neutrality . . . or complicity?

- What does it mean to be a witness? When you've seen something that challenges the accepted narrative, how do you honor it even when it costs you peace?

- How do we heal from being unheard? After your voice has been dismissed or erased, how do you reclaim your story and transform pain into purpose?

What "THE GRASS GROWS WHERE I AM" Means to Me

Wherever I am, resilience is the light and water that transforms my struggles into growth. Even when life felt like only dirt beneath my feet, I discovered that nurturing hope and persistence allows the grass to flourish and be greenest wherever I stand. You are stronger than you know. The seeds of your future are ready to grow.

Lynn Lessell

Connect with Lynn:

From Stressed to Resilience

Lynn Lessell

*The quality of love you share with others
begins with the quality of love you give yourself.*

For most of my life, the idea of putting myself first was utterly foreign to me. Growing up as the oldest of three siblings, I had a mother who made me feel unimportant and neglected, and a father who was emotionally abused, which had left him emotionally distant and absent. Therefore, I was conditioned from a young age to believe that my role, my purpose, was to take care of everyone else.

There were countless little moments that taught me I didn't matter as much as everyone else. I remember waking up at night, a petrified child from a nightmare, running into the kitchen to find my mother sitting at the table, eating spaghetti at midnight. My tears, my fear, were insignificant to her as she looked at me, saying, 'You're fine. Go back to sleep.' Over time, it felt safer to go quiet than to risk being dismissed, so I learned to swallow my words, my needs, and eventually my sense of worth. I wasn't just taking care of everyone else; I was disappearing in the process.

Putting others' needs before my own wasn't just encouraged, it was required. I believed self-focus was not an option. I lived in constant fear of consequences if I dared to break a rule, do anything imperfectly, or do something for myself. I was the perfect people-pleaser, the employee who worked tirelessly to meet everyone else's expectations, the wife and mother who believed her needs came last. I had completely lost touch with my own identity, with what I wanted and needed.

The stress of it all was slowly killing me, but I couldn't see it until I reached a moment when the idea of continuing to live this way felt more painful than the thought of simply not being here to feel anything at all. I remember standing in my bathroom, staring at my reflection, and feeling absolutely hollow behind my eyes, wondering how much longer I could keep pretending I was okay. The thought of untangling the mess of my life, everyone's expectations, my constant people pleasing, and the never-ending to-do lists felt so overwhelming that it seemed easier to keep sleepwalking through my days, even if it was slowly destroying me, than to stop and face the truth of how lost and alone I really felt. In that moment, I wasn't making a plan to end my life, but I also wasn't truly living it; I was merely existing. That realization shook me to my core and became the quiet catalyst for everything that changed next.

When you spend your whole life ignoring your wants and needs, something's got to give. The journey has not been an easy one, nor has it been a quick transformation, but the most significant gain was merging all the "Me's" who exhausted themselves fulfilling the expectations of others into the one person I wanted to be. It's the catalyst that changed my life, allowing me to love myself and everything in it.

What I didn't know then was that losing sight of myself was a gradual process, eroded by subtle daily sacrifices. Somewhere along the way, the girl who used to laugh until tears rolled down her cheeks slowly faded into the background. The curious, kooky, animated part of me, the one who loved to ask questions, tell stories, and be a little silly, got replaced by the version of me who was always "on," always responsible, always composed. I didn't realize it then, but the real Lynn was getting buried under everyone else's expectations, waiting for me to rediscover her.

Over time, I stopped hearing my own voice, opinions, and desires. The more I gave, the less I felt visible, not just to others, but to myself. There were small, almost imperceptible moments of hope along the way. A friend's gentle question, a burst of laughter that caught me off guard, or even time spent alone rekindling a childhood passion, which became stepping-stones back to myself. Recovery wasn't linear or dramatic. Instead, each micro moment of honesty helped me stitch together the version of myself I'd nearly lost. If you recognize pieces of my journey in your own life, know this: Healing starts not in sweeping declarations but in allowing yourself to take up even a little more space each day.

Shift from Stress to Resilience

Many people rush themselves, compare their progress against others, or mistake a misstep for failure. Instead, see every experiment and even every detour as essential learning. There are five roads you'll have to travel to shift from stress to resilience: *review your life's journey, recognize stress, understand your emotional foundation, learn to love and believe in yourself, and redesign the quality lifestyle you desire.* Now here's where you must begin.

Review your life's journey: The road from feeling stressed to resilient looks different for everyone, so there is no set path or amount of time it takes to accomplish it. Suppose you're feeling stressed and chronically overwhelmed while you are looking for steps to repower your resilience. In that case, you'll need to travel down these five separate roads throughout your life to get there. Each one of these roads will have a few different exits, so you'll have to get off to explore various opportunities.

Resilience is not a destination but a continually evolving process requiring patience, courage, and self-compassion. As you travel your unique path, expect detours, moments of uncertainty, and breakthroughs you didn't anticipate. There is no singular "right way" to become resilient. Your experiences, choices, and personality all shape your journey. These "five roads" are guideposts, not rules. At times, you'll need to retrace steps, explore unexpected exits, or spend longer on one path than another. The most important map is your own self-awareness. Some days will feel like progress, while others might seem like setbacks. Give yourself grace; sometimes, revisiting old wounds or obstacles is part of truly moving forward.

Recognizing Stress: Falling into a habit of treating chronic stress as "normal" is as toxic as drinking a glass of poison. You wouldn't intentionally put poison in your body, so why would you permit stress to settle inside and create chaos from the inside out? You can be so busy trying to juggle all the aspects of your life, caring for family, friends, co-workers, and more, while building a successful career to provide for your family, that after an extended period, the invisible stress will begin to eat away at who you want to be until you likely no longer recognize who that person is. You must stop wanting to control everything that happens. You need to start looking for the person who has become buried under all the stress and bring them back to the surface.

What does too much stress look like? It can be different for everyone, and I'll define what it means for me. I regularly ignored myself because of the belief that I was responsible for fulfilling the expectations others had of me. When I realized I was the only one who had a right to have expectations for me to fulfill, things began to change. That realization felt both terrifying and exhilarating. Terrifying, because for the first time I couldn't hide behind what everyone else wanted from me; exhilarating, because it meant I finally had permission to ask, "What does Lynn want?" I remember sitting with that question and feeling completely blank at first, then slowly noticing small desires resurfacing, a quiet walk, a real belly laugh, a moment to breathe without feeling guilty. That was the beginning of reclaiming my identity instead of renting it out to everyone around me.

My life journey was a long one. I had to dig deep to discover who I wanted to be and figure out how to love that person 100 percent. It may sound crazy, but now I'm loving the "me" that's a kooky, animated character who dares to be different; I'm living every day with laughter while presenting someone trustworthy, loyal, and reliable. Everything has gotten better with less stress.

You can't change anything or anyone around you. You must make the change from within and find your identity. That change eventually can restore you to who you are deep down, to allow you to learn how to defuse anxiety. It's not about the awful things you deal with; it's about who you want to be despite them. It's how you bounce back faster. While everyone feels stress, many people overlook the quieter signs: trouble sleeping, snap judgments, aches that don't go away, or a once-light heart that now feels weighted.

Research shows chronic stress doesn't just tax our emotions; it can inflame hearts, disrupt gut health, and exhaust immune systems. I'm proof; my stress gave me it all. Over months and years, the body keeps score even when the mind powers forward. Society rarely rewards pausing for rest or admitting we need help. Instead, we applaud the ones who "hold it together" until they can't. Too often, "just push through" is positioned as a strength. True strength is learning to **pause**, to say "not now" to others when you must say "yes" to yourself, and to notice when you're drinking from that cup of poison.

Understanding your emotional foundation: Just like your physical DNA, I believe you're born with Emotional DNA™: the unique blend of temperament, emotional habits, and resiliency you inherit and acquire shapes every reaction and relationship. Perhaps you grew up in a household where tears were met with dismissal, leading you to learn how to shut down your feelings. Maybe you watched parents cope with stress through anger or withdrawal and unconsciously copied those patterns.

As an adult, you have the power to notice those old scripts and, with support and practice, create new ones. The process begins with gentle awareness, not blame. Your emotions and emotional behavior are cultivated in parts of the brain. In some cases, physical DNA can play a role in making you more susceptible to some behaviors or emotions. If this is a possibility for you, consult a mental health professional to learn more.

Let's get back to Emotional DNA, which I believe is the foundation of who you are. Have you ever noticed that babies seem to have a personality of their own when they are born? No two babies will be the same because DNA from person to person varies. There is even a slight anomaly among identical twins. That's because even though they are born with identical physical DNA, they can have different thoughts and emotions, which lead them on different paths. In other words, they make different choices.

When you're a child, everything seems possible for you. You're curious and try new things without fear of consequences, and you wonder at the discoveries. As a young kid, your resilience is in full gear. You tell others what you want and need. You let others know when you're happy or sad without hesitation until you reach a certain age when what others tell you is right and wrong, and what they expect from you begins to skew how you react. When you succumb to these expectations without questioning what's in your best interest, your inner child may start hiding and become fearful of expressing to others what you want and need. Your ability to bounce back from difficulties can become more challenging. To maintain strong resilience, it's essential to let your internal child help you navigate the external expectations you face as you mature and evaluate how you want to react to them.

Learning to love and believe in yourself: Identity is shaped by many forces: your family, culture, early experiences, and repeated outside feedback. Sometimes, those influences are so subtle or pervasive that you mistake "should" for genuine self-knowledge. When external factors take control of your reactions and resilience levels, causing you to lose track of your foundation, your personality can begin to shift as well. This can affect your sense of self or your identity. If you look in the mirror and feel like a stranger, you're not alone. Most people, at some point, question who they are beneath their roles or accolades.

Have you ever wondered if others perceive you *differently* from how you perceive yourself when you look in a mirror? If you don't see the same person they do, then it may be time to ask what's different, why, and what you can do to change it. If you say to yourself, "There's nothing I can do," then there's something you don't know that you don't know. This tells you it's time to seek out someone who can help you find out what you're unable to see on your own. Identity is shaped not only by your private thoughts but also by the echoes of what others say and believe about you. Many of us compare ourselves to carefully curated images at work, on social media, even in our families, forgetting that what we see is never the whole story. When you can accomplish seeing who you love and believe in when you look in the mirror, you will tap back into your Emotional DNA, revitalize your resilience, and rediscover the person you were meant to be.

Life transitions, such as changing careers, empty nesting, entering new relationships, or moving to a new city, often bring identity into sharper focus. In these moments, old roles fall away, and you're invited to define yourself from the inside out. It's completely normal to feel untethered during these times but remember these are also the moments that offer the greatest opportunity for self-discovery. Identity doesn't develop by keeping to yourself. The people closest to you (such as friends, family, mentors, or even passing acquaintances) can serve as mirrors, sometimes reflecting strengths or qualities you overlook in yourself. Take note of positive feedback or characteristics others consistently mention about you. Are there patterns? What resonates?

Sometimes, others spot a strength or value you haven't fully claimed yet. This is not about letting others define you but about noticing helpful reflections and choosing what you want to keep. When something goes wrong, pause and find one thing you can still control. After a disappointment, make a short list of moments you've come back from before embracing your resilience, even if it feels wobbly. Treat yourself with the gentleness you'd offer to a small child who's fallen: encouragement, patience, and belief in your ability to get up. Resilience grows less from grand recoveries and more from small, repeated acts of self-support and self-respect.

Your sense of self is constantly evolving. The more intentionally you engage in these changes, the more empowered you become to shape a narrative that is truly your own, one that blends both your internal truths and the wisdom gained from your unique journey. Have you ever heard someone say, "Don't worry. Kids bounce back quickly; they're resilient"?

By reclaiming your inner child, you're also reclaiming bountiful resilience. You may be confused about why resilience is such a big deal. Ask yourself, "How quickly do I get happy again after something upsets me?" Do you get over it in minutes or hours, or does it take days, weeks, or months? The old non-resilient me would take years to bounce back from some challenges. Honestly, I never thought I'd forget a single detail of every awful incident. Yet, I've reclaimed who I choose to be with bountiful resilience, and everything has changed for the better.

With your identity and resilience recalibrated to meet your standards, you now must choose what quality looks like in each area of your life. Only you can decide what that should be and make it happen. You don't have to look at all regions simultaneously; however, you should prioritize each category and then tackle them one by one. It won't be easy. I know because I've been through the journey myself, yet with your new understanding of self-worth and self-focus, you'll be able to zig and zag quickly until you find the quality time in that segment of life that suits you. Then you continue the process through each area until you are satisfied with the results.

You can't control other people and all the external factors that come and go, but you have 100 percent control of who you choose to be and how you react. If bouncing back still feels out of reach, that's normal. The speed of your recovery is less important than your willingness to begin again, however messy. Sometimes resilience is just a quiet return to trying, resting, or forgiving yourself, repeatedly. Once you take back control of your identity and resilience, it's time to put that resilience into action to achieve the quality of life you desire. Most people claim to be striving for work-life balance, but it's not possible. It's a myth because you cannot balance unequal parts. The different areas of your life vary in size. The next question becomes, "If I can't achieve balance, how do I achieve a quality lifestyle?"

Redesign the quality lifestyle you desire: After reclaiming your identity and resilience, a new opportunity opens: the freedom to craft a life that genuinely reflects who you are. For years, I chased the myth of perfect balance, measuring my worth by how well I managed to juggle work, family, friendships, health, and everything else. But life isn't made up of equal slices. Each part carries its own weight, and those proportions constantly shift.

The truth is, striving for perfect balance often leaves you feeling like you fall short in every direction. Real quality comes from intentionally choosing what matters most right now, not trying to make all things equal, but making the most important things meaningful. Some weeks, your career may require extra attention; at other times, nurturing relationships, focusing on health, or simply creating space for rest becomes your priority.

Give yourself permission to regularly reevaluate what quality means for you. Don't be afraid to let priorities change. Ask yourself: Where do I feel most depleted? Where do I come alive? Sometimes small shifts like blocking off an hour for solitude, reconnecting with an old friend, leaving work earlier for family time, or setting boundaries around technology can renew your energy and bring your life back into alignment.

It's not about doing more; it's about doing what matters. Being present for moments of joy or stillness, catching yourself when you drift away from your values, and gently redirecting your energy can build a life that feels sustainable and deeply satisfying. Let go of the pressure to achieve some perfect vision of "balance." Instead, try designing a lifestyle that answers your real desires one choice, one day, one meaningful commitment at a time. This is where resilience shows up: not in rigid routines, but in your willingness to listen to yourself, adapt, and honor what you need as life unfolds. When you do, you'll discover a life that feels not just managed but lived. Stress is toxic if you let it take control of your daily life, and this routine can alter your story as you would like it to be written.

Take a Small Action

Here's my challenge to you. I want you to commit, today, to the first small action you can take to prioritize your well-being and start your new journey toward abundant resilience. Whatever it is, I want you to share it with someone who can hold you accountable because you're much more likely to follow through when you put it out there. The true power of resilience lies in its ordinariness. It's found in quiet returns to yourself, incremental acts of courage, and the willingness to be seen both at your strongest and most vulnerable. Every small act of self-respect and consistency nourishes a foundation for the life you're building.

Whatever road you are on, your willingness to keep moving, through setbacks, detours, and days of doubt, means you are already resilient. Your journey is valid. Your growth is real. Consider starting a resilience journal to document your growth, setbacks, and insights. Find an accountability partner, someone to check in with as you take each new step. Remember, community is part of resilience. Don't be afraid to ask for support, whether that means professional help, a friend's listening ear, joining a new social circle, or connecting with me, the Identity Coach.

Take a moment to jot down what resilience looks like for you at your best, and what it looks like on your hardest days. Revisiting what you've read in this chapter can help you measure your own progress beyond what others see. Use tools that help you self-nurture. Picture the tension in your body as a color or weight. Notice where it gathers. With each slow breath, imagine gently loosening its grip, a little more with every exhale. Consider a time you honored a small wish, a walk, a song, or a guilty pleasure program and reflect on how that act of self-honoring made you feel, even if only for a moment. If you find it difficult to ask for help, write down exactly what support you wish for. Even this small act can clarify your needs and help you notice who might be willing, if only you'd let them in. Spend a week jotting down moments when you overreact or go numb. Next to each, ask: "Whose voice am I hearing, mine, or someone from long ago?"

The more you notice, the more choice you reclaim. Think of a recent transition or challenge in your life. How did it shift the way you see yourself? Are there lessons from that change that deserve a place in your identity now? Each morning, face the mirror and look into your eyes. State three words that represent who you want to be today (e.g., "grounded," "open," "compassionate"). In the evening, check in: "Did I act with these qualities? If not, how can I try again tomorrow?"

Today, I'm Lynn Lessell, proudly known as the Identity Coach, helping other high achievers break free from burnout, stress, and self-doubt to master their mindset, build unshakable confidence, and achieve their biggest goals with less stress and more success. The girl who was told, "You're fine, go back to sleep," now helps others wake up to the truth that they matter. If I can do it, you can too!

Reflections for You

- How has prioritizing others' needs impacted your sense of self, and what small step could you take today to reclaim your own voice?

- When you notice stress building in your life, what are the first subtle signs that tell you it's time to pause and check in with yourself?

- What patterns or behaviors from your childhood still influence how you respond emotionally as an adult, and what might you want to change?

- Looking at your reflection in the mirror, do you recognize the person you see? If not, what qualities would you like to nurture moving forward?

- How do you define "quality" in each area of your life, and what is one priority you would like to realign this week?

- Describe a recent situation where your resilience was tested, how did you recover, and what helped you bounce back?

- What does asking for help look like for you, and who might you reach out to as you continue your journey toward greater resilience and self-acceptance?

What "THE GRASS GROWS WHERE I AM" Means to Me

> Many people think that the grass is greener somewhere else. They forget to be grateful for the grass under their own feet. Gratitude is the key to everything because what you focus on expands and we all want more things to be grateful for in our lives.

Dr. Abbey Jo Shulkin

Connect with Dr. Abbey:

From Binge to Balance: A Life Shift in Recovery

Abbey Jo Shulkin

*Weight loss isn't about less of you—
it's about more of the life you were meant to live.*

I really have to laugh when people tell me I have a great body. And they do this often—men and women. If they only knew how I see myself and what I've gone through to look this way, they would be astounded.

Presently, I'm 5'2", weigh 135 pounds, and have a body fat of roughly 24 percent. I wear a very small dress size and look pretty good in a bikini. But it feels as though I'm going through life faking being a thin person. Inside, I don't always feel or think like a thin person at all.

That is probably because I come from a family of women who are obese or have issues with eating and food. As a kid, I watched my mother put on many, many pounds each year until she was morbidly obese. I also saw her fruitless efforts to lose weight and her compulsive eating when my father wasn't home. My mother tried many different weight-loss methods, including the Atkins Diet, diet clubs, a stomach balloon, a liquid-protein fast, and weight-loss retreats. None worked for her.

I thought that people never really lost weight permanently. Even my father's secretary was obese but would occasionally lose 100-plus pounds only to eventually put it back on. I was deathly afraid of becoming fat. My parents' marriage was not happy, and I attributed this mostly to my mother being so overweight. My father, on the other hand, was "normal." Surely they would be happier if my mother wasn't so fat! In my mind, if I was ever going to find a boyfriend, I had better keep my weight down.

Obsession and the Onset of an Eating Disorder

This all sounds like the making of an anorexic, doesn't it? Well, that is only half the story. At the tender age of twelve, I started dieting. At that time, I wasn't thin, nor was I fat. I only thought I was fat. It really annoyed me that I always weighed one pound more than the charts at school recommended. At that age, I was already 5'2" and weighed between 100 and 105 pounds. I know this because I became obsessed with the scale. Every morning, I would stand on that thing. The number displayed would determine how I could feel about myself for the day and how much I could eat.

In particular, I hated my thighs. I remember thinking as a child at summer camp, before I even hit puberty, that if my thighs stayed fat when I became an adult, I was going to take a saw and cut off the fat. (In the 1970s, liposuction wasn't really a thing yet.)

Every day after school, when I was twelve, I swam laps for an hour because I was on the local swim team. This was the year before middle school, and I was becoming aware of boys and desperately wanted them to like me. Swim practice was at dinnertime, so my father made a healthy plate for me to eat afterward. I didn't eat anything from the vending machines or any desserts in an effort to lose weight before junior high. Even with a whole school year of exercise and diet, I didn't see a change. I just still saw fat. This was very frustrating.

Today, there is a term for that called body dysmorphia. This is when you don't see yourself and your body as they actually are or as others see you. Many anorexics have this. We see them as thin as a skeleton, but they believe they are fat, which is why they keep trying to lose weight. This happens the opposite way with obese people. They often avoid mirrors altogether, but when they look, they tell themselves that it's really not all that bad, that they aren't really that fat. The reason for this is that the truth is often too painful to face. This is called denial, a psychological defense mechanism that protects us from the ugly truth. Eating disorders, whether anorexia, bulimia, or compulsive overeating, often go hand in hand with body dysmorphia.

The First Binge and Purge

When I started middle school, I became friends with a girl named Tammy who could eat whatever she wanted and stay thin. It was very frustrating for me to see her eat chocolate every day and remain thinner than me. There I was, obsessively dieting and not losing weight, and there she was, enjoying delicious food and looking fantastic all the time. Life wasn't fair. There was only so much of that I could take, so one day I decided I was going to eat anything and everything that I wanted and would go back to dieting the next day. The dieting didn't work anyhow, I thought, so what's the point?

So, on that one particular day, I ate absolutely everything I wanted. I ended up eating mostly sweets, especially cookies, candies, and ice cream. Pizza, pastas, and hamburgers didn't interest me much if I could have the sweets. I ate so much that day that I was fuller than I had ever been in my life, even fuller than on Thanksgiving or Christmas. The next day, I got on the scale, and it said that I had gained about four pounds! I also felt really sick to my stomach, like there was a rock in it.

For a distraction, I went outside to meet up with some of the neighbor kids. One young man, who I had a crush on, offered me a ride on the back of his bike. Normally I would have been thrilled, but I felt like my bloated stomach made me look six-months pregnant. I couldn't even sit comfortably on that bike. My only thought was that I needed to get rid of all that food in my stomach as quickly as possible.

Off I went to the local store where I purchased a box of laxatives. Of course, they were the chocolate kind. Immediately after leaving the store, I ate a few, but when they didn't work quickly enough, I proceeded to eat a few more, and then a few more before bed. All of this was done without consulting an adult. That night I didn't sleep much because I spent most of my time on the toilet with a severe case of diarrhea. This was the official beginning of my eating disorder, which I will call BED (binge eating disorder) and bulimia, the binge-purge syndrome.

Escalation and Desperation

Purging can take on many forms, as it did in me. During my time as a bulimic, I tried almost every method of purging, including restricting food intake, self-induced vomiting, chemically induced vomiting, laxatives, and excessive exercise. My eating disorder started in 1976 when terms like *bulimia*, *eating disorder*, and *treatment center* weren't known to most people. I had an eating disorder, though, even though I didn't know exactly what it was.

I thought that this food binge was a one-time thing. I wasn't planning on repeating it anytime soon, especially the laxative part. To my consternation, though, I began binging regularly. At first it was once a month. Then it occurred every two weeks, then every week, and eventually every other day, and finally almost every day. This happened over nine years.

I never knew when the obsessive thought to binge would get in my head. Sometimes it was after school, and sometimes it was on the weekend. I had little to no control over it. Every time I binged, I promised myself that I would never do it again. I would try to analyze why I did it, always blaming something or somebody outside myself. When I did conclude that it was my weak character, I would mentally beat myself up over it. During the time that I was an active bulimic, my self-esteem sunk to extremely low levels.

The ways I tried to control my weight after binging were numerous. I even tried some drugs and alcohol to stop myself from eating. Because I rarely ate around other people, I did strange things like trying to be around others just so I wouldn't binge. When they wanted to have a meal, I would leave so I wouldn't have to eat the fattening food they were eating, but then I would feel lonely and deprived and binge anyhow.

I also thought that having a boyfriend would solve all my problems, especially the food one. The only obsession that rivaled food was the one I had with boys. This desperation for a boyfriend was not very healthy or good for my social life or reputation. The harder I tried to snag one, the more a relationship seemed to elude me. When I felt rejected by a young man, my first way of consoling myself was with food, of course. I thought they rejected me because I was too fat, so when I binged and got fatter, I only drove myself further away from my goal of finding love. This made me so depressed that I attempted suicide.

Crisis and Attempted Therapy

One day I was so depressed and obsessed with the two half-gallons of ice cream in the freezer at home that I went to the school nurse to get permission to leave, claiming I was sick. I must have looked pretty bad, even though nothing was really wrong with me. At this point in my life, I was getting on the scale daily. I knew that if I ate that ice cream in the freezer, I would gain so much weight that I couldn't get it off before the weekend. I would rather be dead than fat, so I decided to put poison on the ice cream before eating it, hoping to die.

I ended up going to a hospital where I drank something that made me vomit up the ice cream and poison. I was relieved that I didn't gain weight. This was the first time I told anybody about my obsession with my weight and eating. The hospital recommended that I get some help, so I started to see a psychiatrist and a social worker.

The suicide attempt happened when I was fourteen. For the next seven years, I went to all kinds of therapists to try to get rid of my binge eating. It didn't help at all. As a matter of fact, my binge eating got progressively worse. From the outside, nobody knew that I had an eating disorder, but I knew it, and I was not in denial. I just didn't know how to get rid of it. The fact that I thought I was fat was not so bothersome, but the bizarre binge eating and starving were making me miserable, and I was unable to stop.

Exercise and College Decline

Although neither of my parents were into sports, for some reason they put me in tap-dancing lessons when I was three. From there I moved on to ballet and some gymnastics. My first ballet teacher was a tall, willowy, young, blond British woman who was a former member of the British Royal Ballet. In her class at the tender age of five, I learned how to stretch. This began my love of exercise. I hoped that when I grew up, I would look like that ballet teacher. To this day, I'm still waiting for this to happen.

I continued with ballet, going twice a week until I was thirteen. The plumpness of my body made me realize that I could never make a career out of dancing, so eventually I stopped. At one point my mom bought me an exercise booklet, at my request, when we were at the checkout at the local drugstore. This book was called *How to Reduce Hips and Thighs*. It had pictures and exercises that targeted those areas. During summer vacations, I would get up in the morning, put on some music, and do all the exercises in the book. I did this every day out of my own free will because I thought that if I didn't do anything about my body, it wouldn't change, and I was not okay with the way it was.

In junior high school, when my binge eating became more frequent, I decided to counteract it with exercise. Luckily, the local YMCA offered group exercise classes that I attended almost every day. It gave me the feeling that I was at least doing something. I was the youngest person in the class. I also taught myself how to jog. Jogging was just starting to be the rage back in the late seventies. It was a common sight in my town to see the mayor and a group of others running along the rural roads trying to stay fit. When I started, I ran from my house to the end of the block. I did this a few days in a row before I decided to go to the end of the next block. Slowly I built up my distance one block at a time until I could run ten miles without stopping. I did this not out of a love for the sport, but purely to lose the weight I put on during my food binges. The only issue was that after a ten-mile jog I needed to eat again, so I'm not sure that it helped me lose weight. It kept me out of the kitchen for a little while, though.

I went off to college, and all exercise stopped due to lack of time. I still made time to binge and purge, though. When my brother came to visit during my first vacation week, he said that he had never seen me so fat. This crushed me. It was probably true because I no longer had the social control of living with my parents to stop me from overeating. I also was living in a new city where I knew nobody and had a lot of pressure academically and socially. This combination exacerbated my eating disorder. The harder I tried to control my eating and lose weight, the more weight I seemed to gain.

Recognizing Addiction in New York

Obviously, I was very sick. I knew it but didn't know what to do. Therapy didn't work for me, and diets didn't help because I couldn't stick to them. Exercise only put a small dent in my enormous calorie consumption during a binge. My solution was to move to New York City. There I wouldn't be lonely because there were so many people and so much to do. That would stop me from binging, I thought. Well, it didn't. I felt even lonelier than before!

One day after binging and purging in the communal bathroom in the college dorms, another student approached me and asked if I was all right. Not caring anymore if people knew my deep, dark secret about my insane eating behaviors, I told her about them. To my surprise, she told me that she had done that too but had gotten help and was doing fine now. This was the first person I ever met who had gotten off the hellish eating disorder merry-go-round.

She referred me to a clinic she had gone to, which was in New York City. I started seeing a counselor there. Every time I went, I cried my eyes out. Every single time! My therapist there was a recovered heroin addict. She helped me see my eating problem as an addiction. I ate the way alcoholics drank and the way drug addicts used dope. It was all about sneaky behaviors and scoring a fix. This made sense to me. It wasn't about my weak will or gluttony. I was addicted to food, especially sugary food and in particular chocolate.

My addictions weren't only to food, though. I had picked up the habit of smoking marijuana to stop my mind from obsessing about food for a little while. Looking back, I see that smoking weed only made my eating disorder worse. It lowered my blood sugar, which gave me the infamous "munchies," and it added to my distorted perception of myself.

Alcohol was also an issue for me. Every time I drank, from the very first time, I drank like an alcoholic. Once I started, I couldn't stop. Before going out to a bar I would tell myself that I would only have two drinks due to their calorie content. I could never stick to this. I would often lose count at twelve or more. I drank until I puked or passed out. It's dangerous for a young woman to be out of control drunk in public. Luckily, I decided not to drink anymore because of the calories. Having an eating disorder actually saved me from becoming a full-blown, low-bottom alcoholic. Many of the people that I hung out with then did end up that way.

The therapist at the clinic in the city told me that if I wanted to get over the eating problem, I would have to stop smoking marijuana, using other drugs, and drinking. I didn't believe her. I didn't see the drug use as an issue; the eating was my issue. Surely I could still keep toking. I only wanted to be rid of the strange eating behaviors.

Therapeutic Community and Recovery Discipline

After four months of outpatient treatment while attending a prestigious design school in New York City, I was admitted as a full-time, live-in patient at a therapeutic community (a fancy name for a rehab) in New York City. That was on February 2, 1986. Everyone there was a recovering addict or alcoholic, or just "crazy." Some were "double trouble" with both an addiction and an eating disorder. Only a few people were there solely for an eating disorder. At the time there were not as many treatment centers as there are now.

I thought treatment centers were only for the rich and famous. My family sacrificed much to be able to send me there. My grandmother realized that it was either that or I wouldn't have been alive for much longer. My first weekend there was traumatic. I felt like I had checked myself into an asylum. This was a new bottom for me.

The hardest part was having to eat with everybody, especially the young men. I had tried to keep this secret hidden from any male. I thought they would run away screaming if they knew how crazy and sick I was. I didn't realize I was actually sick, though, at the time. I thought I was a bad person with no self-control.

I was attracted to some of the male patients, so eating in front of them was very scary. Of course, at the beginning I tried all kinds of ways of getting out of this, such as refusing to go to meals, leaving the clinic, and eating secretly. Eventually, I straightened out and went to meals and tried to eat normally. It might have looked normal on the outside, but what my head was telling me about what I should and should not eat was definitely not normal. I did get in the habit of eating three meals a day and not eating any sugar. Also, I broke my addiction to diet soda there.

They made us keep our rooms clean along with the rest of the house. It was a bit like being in bootcamp. When we weren't in therapy, we were cleaning. They said the condition of your underwear drawer and house reflects your state of mind. If my house is organized and clean, there is a big chance I will stay organized and clean from my drug of choice, food. If my house is messy, dirty, and chaotic, there is a big chance that I am like that too, especially in my mind.

That is why to this day I make my bed every day before leaving the house, and I periodically organize my closets and cupboards. My mind is at rest when my house is in order, and there is much less chance of me having a "slip" with food than when I'm a chaotic, out-of-control mess.

Last Steps to Sobriety and New Life

Even though I changed, learned a lot, and recovered a great deal while living in that therapeutic community, I still wasn't one hundred percent sober in my eating practices. I still craved chocolate and binged when I moved out.

When the binging became more frequent again, I decided to go to a twelve-step program where I received much help. It took me many months of working the twelve-step program before I became sober in my eating practices. It happened in the spring of 1988 when I was a student in Paris.

When I first became sober in my eating practices, I couldn't believe it. I was just waiting for the moment that I was going to slip up and binge. My new way of eating and living felt so fragile. I just tried to get through each day, one day at a time.

After a few months without bingeing, the universe saw fit for me to finally meet a quality man. He happened to be from the Netherlands, which is why after I graduated from college, I moved to The Hague and became his wife. Early in our relationship, I told him about my eating disorder, and he was very understanding. He tried very hard to help me with it by cooking for me and encouraging me to go to the local gym, which helped me feel better about my body.

Eventually I gave birth to two healthy girls. During each pregnancy, I gained a nominal amount of weight and was back in my jeans within a week. Because my mind is not full of thoughts about my weight and food all day, I have been able to do things that I never thought were possible for me. One of them was returning to school and becoming a doctor of acupuncture and Chinese medicine. This enables me to help others become the healthiest version of themselves.

The Life Shifts System

And today at sixty years old and having maintained the same weight and clothing size for over thirty-five years, I love nothing more than first teaching and then helping my patients implement the Life Shifts Weight Wellness system. This is a system I developed from my hard-earned life knowledge that helps individuals finally achieve and maintain their healthiest body size by undergoing a multilayered lifestyle makeover. This unique system gets to the root cause of the weight problem and teaches people how to live without ever having to diet again.

I don't believe that the next fad diet, workout plan, carb-tracking app, weight-loss injection, or even bariatric surgery are the answer. They do not teach new habits and are not sustainable. They also don't get to the root cause. Therapy alone without new eating habits doesn't work either. What is needed is to make one change, and that is to change everything.

The Shifts That Changed My Life— And Can Change Yours

The most powerful transformations I've made—and now help my clients make—started with adding structure to life. Structure doesn't create restriction; it creates freedom. Once I began organizing not just my meals but my days, my energy and focus returned, and my mind stopped spinning around food and weight.

I also committed to rigorous honesty—with myself and others. Honesty keeps me out of denial and helps me face life instead of hiding from it. When we tell ourselves the truth, fear begins to fade, and healing begins to happen.

Another shift came from moving my body with purpose and joy. I no longer exercise just to control my weight—I move because it boosts my mood, balances my hormones, and builds self-confidence. Movement became medicine for both my body and mind.

I learned that lasting results come from consistency, not intensity. I stopped chasing quick fixes and instead focused on finishing what I start. Progress may be slow, but it's steady—and that's where the magic happens.

One of the hardest but most liberating changes was letting go of control. When I was in the depths of my eating disorder, I believed everything had to go my way or it would fall apart. Today, I allow life to unfold. I don't force outcomes, especially in relationships.

The result? More peace, more connection, and more genuine friendships than I ever imagined.

I also stopped saying "yes" when I meant "no." I no longer do things just to please others. Now I do what's right for me, because self-respect invites respect.

Perhaps the biggest mindset shift was retiring my inner judge. I realized that everyone, including me, is doing the best they can with the tools they have. Compassion replaced criticism, and gratitude became my daily anchor.

And, finally, the most life-changing shift of all: I stopped trying to control my eating and weight. Instead, I created a structured food plan that brings balance and peace. I don't wonder what or when to eat—I simply follow my plan, and my mind is free to focus on living.

Each of these shifts built upon the last, creating a foundation for lasting transformation. They gave me a life beyond my wildest dreams. If you had told my 21-year-old self that I'd one day live with freedom, health, and purpose, I would have laughed. But now I know the truth: dreams come true and miracles happen—when we're willing to make the shifts that change everything.

"If nothing changes then nothing changes."
—SOURCE UNKNOWN

REFLECTIONS FOR YOU

- What have you already done to control your eating and your weight? What's worked, what hasn't, and why?

- How much of your mental and emotional energy is spent thinking about food, your body, or the scale each day? And how would your life feel if that energy were freed up?

- What areas of your life—such as organization, relationships, mindset, or self-care—might be connected to your struggles with food and weight? Can you see how shifting these layers could change everything?

- When you "slip" with food or your goals, how do you usually respond to yourself? Do you show compassion, or do you fall into guilt and self-criticism?

- What fears or beliefs might be keeping you from achieving lasting freedom from food and weight struggles? What do you tell yourself about what's possible—or not possible—for you?

- What would your ideal relationship with food, your body, and your health look and feel like six months from now? Describe the version of you who has already made that shift.

- Are you ready to stop dieting and start transforming your life—one small, consistent shift at a time?

Connect with Dr. Abbey:

What "THE GRASS GROWS WHERE I AM" Means to Me

> *The grass truly grows where we pour our love, our courage, and our commitment. And for me, that means choosing every day to water women, children, and the future itself.*

Tina Vaida

Connect with Tina:

Empowering Women and Children: Wisdom, Strength, and Global Impact

Tina Vaida

Resilience is not about enduring the storm but becoming the light that guides others through it.

Growth, transformation, and resilience do not just happen for anyone by coincidence or accident; rather, they are intentional as you grow in wisdom and strength, ultimately leading to global impact. Leaning into empowering women and children by providing them with skills, education, and resources while fostering entrepreneurship and attracting groups to come together creates a sense of belonging and social bonds while watering the spirit to grow. Focusing on empowering women and children creates a healthier environment by promoting sustainable practices leading to healthier communities. This fosters pride that leads to enhancing resilience and the quality of life. These elements occur where we choose to nurture, protect, and empower those around us. By nurturing the wisdom and strength of children and women, societies can unlock their full potential, leading to transformation in the world at large.

Just as the grass grows where it is watered, so, too, do people flourish when given the right support, knowledge, and opportunities. For too long, society has placed limitations on women and children, shaping their paths with unrealistic and outdated expectations, stereotypes, and challenges meant to confine rather than liberate. Likewise, many men have lost their way, disconnected from their true potential being led by outdated societal norms that tell them they must be "unbreakable" rather than vulnerable, powerful rather than self-aware. In a global world that constantly evolves, women and children stand at the forefront of a social, economic, and cultural transformation. Their struggles, resilience, and unwavering strength have not only shaped their own lives but have also influenced societies across the globe. From early childhood, when gender norms and societal expectations begin shaping identity to adulthood, when barriers and limitations are imposed, women and young people navigate a unique challenging path that often comes with labels, judgments, and expectations. Indeed, it is precisely within these challenges that they uncover their true strength, wisdom, and ability to transform not only their own lives but also the world around them.

At the core of this journey lies a profound truth: Life is not just about personal success but about the impact we have on others and the people we uplift, empower, and inspire. The wisdom passed down by generations of women before us is not just advice; it is a foundation of strength, creativity, and an unyielding drive for global change. It is a sacred inheritance, an energy that courses through us, urging us to rise beyond adversity, challenge the norms, and create a future where women and children thrive. Just as grass grows where it is watered, the future flourishes where we nurture it. Women and children are the seeds of our collective future, and it is our duty to cultivate their growth, ensuring that they are not only protected but truly empowered. When we water the roots of resilience, education, and opportunity, the next generation will rise stronger, greener, and more vibrant than ever before. I believe that behind every powerful woman and every resilient child lies a story of courage, determination, and the refusal to be defined by limitations. Strength is not measured by moments of triumph alone but by the ability to rise from the ashes of struggle, transformed and more powerful than before.

Hardship Forges Resilience

Life has tested me in ways that could have broken my spirit, yet each hardship became a refining fire and moments that forged within me an unshakable resilience. Like a diamond formed under immense pressure, I emerged stronger, brighter, and more determined to illuminate the path for myself and others. My journey, like so many of you, is a testament to the fact that we are not defined by the obstacles we face but by how we rise above them.

My journey of resilience is deeply rooted in Transylvania, a land of ancient wisdom, folklore, and untamed beauty. Born amidst its mystical landscapes, I inherited the echoes of a lineage steeped in strength and tradition. Raised by my grandmother, who was a woman of immense strength, wisdom, and unwavering spirit, I learned early on that power is not bestowed; it is something cultivated from within. My grandmother was a healer, a practitioner of natural medicine and witchcraft, and a keeper of artisanal knowledge. She taught me the value of resilience, self-reliance, and creativity and equipped me with practical skills that became the foundation of my empowerment. She introduced me to the world of natural medicine, the artistry of sewing, and the power of embracing one's inner magic. All these elements became symbols of survival and strength in a world overshadowed by communism.

More than that, she instilled in me the courage to dream beyond the limitations imposed by the external world. She taught me that even in the darkest times, even when the world seeks to confine you, the spirit of a woman can remain unbreakable, soaring beyond oppression, beyond fear, beyond expectations. This resilience, forged in my earliest years, became my guiding force as I migrated to new countries, built my name in the fiercely competitive world of fashion, and found my voice as a leader, creator, and advocate for women and children. My journey has mirrored the journeys of countless women worldwide, women who have risen above obstacles, transcended societal limitations, and reclaimed their voices.

I believe that women must embrace their struggles and allow these experiences to become stepping-stones toward their own greatness. It is essential for women and children everywhere to understand that their hardships are not signs of weakness but proof of their immense power. Just as grass grows where we water it, empowerment flourishes where we invest in it. If we fail to nurture the voices, dreams, and potential of women and children, we allow the world to remain barren. But when we pour into them, providing love, education, opportunity, and safety, they bloom into forces that reshape the world. Breaking barriers is the universal journey of women and children in my experience.

*Every word we speak, every silence we keep,
shapes the soil where the future grows.*

Define Your Self-Worth

Throughout my travels and international experiences, I have met young girls and boys facing the same struggles I once had, whether it is battling for self-worth, navigating societal expectations, or fighting against the pressures to conform. Whether facing poverty, a lack of education, or relentless judgment, every child who overcomes adversity carries an unbreakable spirit. We must honor these journeys. We must create spaces where women and children feel protected, respected, and free to embrace their full selves. The rise of one woman, the rise of one child, should be a call to action for all. Their success is not an isolated victory; it is a ripple effect that can shift the very foundation of society.

When I co-authored *From Startup to Stand Out* with Kevin Harrington from *Shark Tank*, I shared the very lessons that shaped my journey on how resilience and adaptability, and the courage to forge your own path are the true keys to success. My path in the fashion industry was not a conventional one; I built my brand, not just as a business, but as a movement, a vision, and a force for global change. Success, whether in business, personal growth, or advocacy, is not about where you start but rather it is about how you rise, what you nurture, and the impact you make. This is the philosophy that guides everything I do and the core mission of VAIDA WORLD.

I was immediately drawn to the co-authorship with Noah Crane when I read the title of the book, *The Grass Grows Where I Am*. This speaks to the idea that wherever we are, we can cultivate growth, beauty, and wisdom. The empowerment of women and children is not a singular act but a collective movement that touches every part of society. From the wisdom of our grandmothers to the lessons we teach our own daughters and sons, women are the torch bearers of knowledge, resilience, and strength. But this movement is not just about individual empowerment; it is about building a world where every woman and every child is valued, protected, and given the space to rise. Yet, rising alone is not enough. We must build a world where strength does not come at the cost of injustice or suffering. Women and children should not be forced to endure their struggles in silence. I have come to know that the principles of "Elevate & Empowerment" form the foundation of progress for women and children. Therefore, I have committed myself to educating and inspiring others through a global initiative focused on fostering empowerment, mental health awareness, and the celebration of inner strength and self-worth.

From an early age, children absorb the messages society imposes on them. Girls are often told they are "too much" or "not enough" while boys are discouraged from expressing emotions. These toxic narratives create insecurity and self-doubt, leading to lifelong struggles with identity and mental health issues. Together, we can change this. We must empower the next generation—the future of humanity, our children—to define their own identity and self-worth. We must not adhere to society's standards but rather embrace the values defined by ourselves. As a result, my company, VAIDA, has evolved beyond the conventional boundaries of a fashion house to become a catalyst for empowerment and inclusion.

While fashion has often been seen as a superficial industry, I have redefined it as a platform for positive transformation integrating empowerment, sustainability, and holistic well-being. From the moment I founded the brand of VAIDA WORLD, my commitment has extended beyond aesthetics, to fostering a deeper purpose. VAIDA embodies values of integrity, community, and conscious innovation, encouraging women and children to embrace their roots, their creativity, and their unique stories to make a positive impact on the world. More than just a label, VAIDA is a movement, continuously expanding its global influence and reshaping the industry with consciously purpose-driven fashion. Every piece I create is infused with purpose.

My collections are designed not merely to adorn the body but to empower the soul. Through my work, I have redefined fashion as a tool for change while partnering with charities, while advocating for women and children, and while establishing new benchmarks for ethical and sustainable production. Fashion holds the power to heal, to empower, and to create a better future. For this reason, VAIDA is at the forefront of that revolution. As the CEO of VAIDA, I have committed to this global change by designing garments that embrace confidence, uniqueness, individuality, and strength. By collaborating with charities worldwide, I support initiatives that create sustainable solutions and uplift women and children. My efforts and initiative ensure that every project I undertake has a direct, meaningful impact on those in need, fostering holistic empowerment. The change starts from within each one of us, at the grassroots level, expanding outward to create a ripple effect that transforms individuals, communities, and society.

The Children Are Our Future

The grass grows where we water it. The future thrives where we nurture it, and women and children are the seeds of tomorrow. By cultivating their strength, resilience, and opportunities, we can shape a world that is more empowered, vibrant, and inclusive than ever before. Together, we can drive lasting transformation. Together, we can change the world. One empowered life at a time. I feel it is so important for women and young people everywhere to understand that their struggles are not a sign of weakness but a testament to their own power. The young women and people that I meet while traveling the world are challenged by the same troubles. Every challenge they face, every barrier they break, and every judgment they overcome is a testament to their unbreakable spirit. We must honor these journeys, embrace our strength and continue to rise, despite the weight of the world.

I have come to learn that women, children, and young people are not just individual figures of strength; they are also architects of the future. Their resilience, wisdom, and capacity to build communities are the foundations of a better world. To truly rise, we must create spaces where they feel protected, respected, and free to express their full selves. But strength and resilience should not come at the cost of injustice or harm. We must recognize that while women can rise above their struggles, they should not be forced to face them alone, nor should they endure them in silence.

The truth is, society has a responsibility, a moral obligation, to protect and respect women, children, and young adults at all costs. They cannot be left to fight their battles alone. Just as a community raises a child, so must society raise women up by supporting them, protecting them, watering them, and creating an environment where they can thrive without fear of judgment or harm. This is not just a question of ethics but a measure of our society's health and progress. Judgment can erode your sense of self-worth, leading to confusion, insecurity, and mental health challenges.

In a world that criticizes and confines, we must empower young girls and boys to know their value, not by society's standards, but by their own. That beauty lies within, not on the outside. The ability to shine in their confidence is what truly makes them beautiful and strong. They must be taught that their beauty and strength lie not in how others perceive them but in how they see themselves. Their strength lies in their ability to define their own path, set their own boundaries, and stand firm in their worth. The clothing I design for people of every age embraces their unique talents to shine, feel confident, and step into their own power to create impact and change on a local and global scale. The charities I partner with at events all around the world speak to empowering young girls and boys.

Creating a platform for all to win is the mission of VAIDA WORLD, and the collaboration gives all involved a chance to grow and transform. We must teach our girls and boys from a young age that their worth is not defined by the labels others place on them. Being beautiful or confident does not make a girl any less deserving of respect, just as being assertive does not make them bossy or difficult. Likewise, we must teach our boys and young men that strength is not about suppressing their emotions or hiding their struggles. True masculinity is not measured by silence, or toughness alone, but by courage to express, to feel, and to be vulnerable without fear of judgment. Sensitivity, compassion, and self-awareness are signs of strength, not weakness.

We must educate children and young adults on the importance of mental health, emotional intelligence, and resilience, helping them to understand that it is okay to struggle sometimes, to seek support, and to embrace their full humanity. No one's worth is defined by outdated stereotypes or by anyone's opinions. Men, too, face their own battles, many unspoken. They are often told to suppress emotions, to be strong even when they feel lost, and to push forward without acknowledging pain. But true strength comes from embracing one's journey, rediscovering one's path, and learning to grow again. Resilience is the foundation for transformation.

VAIDA WORLD is more than a philosophy; it is a movement of conscious empowerment. It is the belief that, no matter where we are, we can nurture, uplift, and create lasting change. This is not just about personal success; it is about fostering an ecosystem of growth where people of all backgrounds can thrive. Mental health is one of the most overlooked yet critical aspects of a child and young person's well-being. In a fast-paced world filled with expectations, social media pressures, and academic demands, children are more vulnerable than ever to anxiety, depression, and self-doubt. Children are the heartbeat of the future. They will inherit the world we build today. We must prioritize their mental health, education, and opportunities so that they grow up knowing they can stand tall, dream big, and lead with confidence.

Through VAIDA WORLD, I am committed to providing opportunities, mentorship, and empowerment to the next generation, ensuring that they step into the world with unshakable confidence. A child's mind is the soil in which their future is planted. If that soil is filled with self-doubt, anxiety, and pressure, how can we expect them to grow into confident, empowered individuals? Through VAIDA WORLD, I have made it a priority to integrate mental health awareness and education into our initiatives and community work. It is not enough to dress children in beautiful clothes; we must ensure they have the confidence, education, and emotional support they need to navigate life. Education is not just about academics; it is about teaching children to value themselves, their voices, and their potential to be kind and resilient. The future of fashion, of business, and of society depends on how we nurture the next generation, encompassing mental, emotional, and intellectual health.

If my journey resonates with you, if you believe in empowerment, transformation, and the power of fashion as a force for change, then I invite you to be part of that mission by collaborating with VAIDA. This is more than just a mission; it's a movement. A movement to break barriers, redefine standards, and create a world where confidence, authenticity, and strength belong to everyone. Together, we can shape a future where fashion is not just about aesthetics but about impact. Advocating for sustainability, inclusiveness, and meaningful and resilient change. Whether you are an individual ready to step into your power, a business striving for conscious innovation, a charity amplifying voices, or a community organization creating waves of impact, your role is vital. Let's unite our visions, amplify our influence, and build something that lasts beyond trends and transforms lives. The time for change is now. Let's work together to inspire, uplift, and set a new global standard for empowerment, resilience, and purpose. Book me for speaking engagements to inspire and empower your communities.

*Where roots of love meet the light of purpose—
the world blooms.*

VAIDA WORLD—Empowering women and children, one seed of change at a time.

Closing Reflection

The more we reflect, the more we awaken the quiet truth that transformation begins within us—and ripples outward. Every act of kindness, every seed of empowerment, and every moment of courage plants roots that will one day bloom in someone else's garden. We are all gardeners of the future, shaping a world where women rise without fear, where children grow without limits, and where compassion becomes our shared language. The grass truly grows where it is watered—and together, we are the ones holding the watering can.

Reflections for You

- How have the hardships you've faced shaped the way you now define strength, resilience, and self-worth?

- What does true empowerment mean to you—not just for yourself, but for those whose lives you quietly touch? How do you use your voice, your kindness, your courage to make others feel seen?

- How can we, as a global community, better uplift women and children to rise into their full potential? What shifts in mindset, opportunity, or compassion are needed for every voice to be heard?

- In what ways can your own story—personal or professional—become a platform for change? What message does your journey whisper to those who will come after you?

- What outdated beliefs or inherited limitations are you ready to release in order to rise freer and stronger?

- How can you "water the grass" where you stand—in your family, your work, or your community—so that others may bloom too?

What "THE GRASS GROWS WHERE I AM" Means to Me

" *I'm planted, right where I am. Instead of constantly wishing for another season, place, or circumstance, I can lean into where God has me now, and allow my spirit to grow roots of faith, resilience, and joy in this soil.* "

Tami Wellman

Connect with Tami:

Cultivating a Garden of Faith: Thriving Where You're Planted

Tami Lynn Wellman

They will be like a tree planted by the water that sends out its roots by the stream. It does not fear when heat comes; its leaves are always green.

—Jeremiah 17:8 (NIV)

At forty, everything fell apart. I never imagined that midlife would come with so much pain, uncertainty, and isolation. I was the woman people came to for answers, encouragement, direction, and spiritual strength. I had led ministries, built businesses, coached and mentored others, and raised a beautiful family. I knew what it was like to pour my heart into something, to fight for it, and to see it grow. I believed those years had built unshakable stability. But suddenly, I found myself walking through one of the most disorienting seasons of my life. I was stuck in what felt like a never-ending nightmare.

My life had been flipped upside down. I was kicked into fight-or-flight mode, and survival became my constant companion. Sleep became a stranger. My mind spun relentlessly, overthinking, overanalyzing, trying to make sense of what made no sense at all. Every day was a blur of hard decisions, carrying the full weight of financial stability, emotional safety, and spiritual guidance for me and my four girls. I could not simply hold on. I had to figure it out. I had to lead through my own storm while holding the hands of four young women who were looking to me for stability, comfort, and hope.

When you are in ministry and your marriage falls apart, regardless of the reason, people scatter fast. The support system you thought you had suddenly evaporates. Friends do not know what to say. Invitations stop. The phone that once rang with requests for your help is silent when you are the one in need. I was left alone to navigate the wreckage of divorce. My identity as a wife was gone. My career and my community were gone as well. It is like falling off a cliff and landing on a small ledge, or being dropped in a desert without food, water, or shelter, left to survive with your skills alone. The silence is deafening except for the sound of your pounding heart and racing thoughts.

It is a strange and painful thing to have spent your life building community, extending love and acceptance to others in tough seasons, only to discover that when it is your turn, many will quietly step back. I understood on some level. People are often afraid of change, afraid of pain, and sometimes unable to separate your situation from their own discomfort. But understanding did not make it hurt less.

Anchored in Faith

I realized something I have always known, while I run toward people in pain, most people run away. I am not one to freeze or give up when I am knocked down. I am also not one to let fear or confusion dictate my next move. I am oddly comfortable in uncomfortable situations, so even when I did not know what was next or how to get there, I knew each day would bring the next step. I am deeply grateful for the mentors, coaches, and valuable life experiences that gave me tools long before I knew I would desperately need them. These tools became daily lifelines and a compass in my storm. But they were not my anchors. My anchor was, and still is, my faith.

The tools gave me a way forward. My faith in God gave me the courage to take the next step. My natural mind wanted to protect me, and my emotions wanted me to curl up in a ball and wait for rescue, but I knew no one was coming to save me in the way I imagined. God was with me, yes, but I still had to get up and move. I was a grown woman and a mother of four girls who needed me to lead them. They needed me to handle my healing without adding to theirs. They needed my daily presence, guidance, comfort, and encouragement.

So, I put one foot in front of the other. I worked three jobs to keep a roof over their heads and food on the table. I found comfort in doing small acts of kindness, baking cookies, hosting pasta parties, attending soccer games, watching movies, helping with homework, driving them to friends' houses, and nursing them through sickness. I had always taught my girls that when you do not know what to do, you serve your way out. I wanted to model resilience, faith, and hope.

By the grace of God, each day I grew more confident, clearer, and more joyful, and slowly a new, better life emerged.

Tools to Rebuild a Life of Purpose

Years before my personal life unraveled, I had been creating the tools to walk through my current season; these would become valuable tools and a lifeline when I had the bottom fall out, was disoriented, and needed something to hold onto and build a new life with. I realized that the crisis revealed my gifts, those that I didn't realize I had but were transferable to my next chapter of life and would only get stronger as I used them. For me that was church planting, coaching competitive soccer, raising four girls, and going back to graduate school at thirty-eight years old.

At twenty-six years old with three young children, my husband and I packed up our family and moved to the Northeast to plant a church and support dozens of others that grew out of that decision. Church planting is not for the faint of heart. It means starting with nothing but a God-given vision and the conviction to see it through. That experience taught me to think strategically under pressure, to lead with compassion, to delegate wisely, and to keep showing up even when the results are not immediate.

As a nationally licensed soccer coach and former collegiate player, I learned to play out of pressure, to reset after mistakes, and to trust my training. Coaching athletes taught me endurance, discipline, and mental toughness. These hard-earned skills became lifelines off the field.

Parenting four daughters taught me to lead with intentionality, consistency, and grace. I became their life coach, guiding them through challenges and celebrating their victories. I learned how to be present, courageous, compassionate, and confident, building a legacy of faith that would live beyond me.

Graduate school counseling at age thirty-eight stretched me even further. I was running a nonprofit for women's health, raising four kids, and keeping up with demanding academics, all while participating in personal counseling myself. It was exhausting, but it taught me the value of self-reflection, deep listening, seeking wise counsel, and pursuing growth even when the path was difficult. I learned that I could be a healer even as I was still healing.

When we face life challenges, loss of income, divorce, health crisis, we already have the tools to respond and rebuild. We just need to look for them, remind ourselves of the support within, and take the action forward. The next steps will rise to meet us. New support systems, new skills, and better opportunities are often on the other side of heartbreak. A devastating low is often a redirection from God to a better relationship, career, or calling. The challenge reveals that your circumstance is too small to support your destiny, and the re-direction is an invitation to outgrow your old life and step into your best life.

Looking back, I can see that all these experiences, including ministry, leadership, sports, parenting, and graduate school, were preparation. They gave me four tools that would become essential when my life hit its lowest point. The first tool was learning to act before I had it all figured out. Too often, we wait until we have every answer before making a move, but momentum is often what brings clarity. I learned to start where I was, with what I had, trusting God to meet me along the way. The second tool was the ability to reset and refocus quickly. On the soccer field, you cannot let one bad play define the game. In life, you cannot let one setback define the rest of your life. I learned to shake it off, breathe, pray, and get back in the game. The third tool was the discipline of being fully present for the people who needed me most. My daughters did not need a perfect mother, they needed a present one. I learned that showing up consistently, even in small ways, builds trust, stability, and hope. The fourth tool was the power of creating an environment for daily growth. This meant building small, consistent habits; reading Scripture in the morning, journaling gratitude, moving my body, preparing healthy food, speaking life over myself, and service to others.

From Buried to Planted

These daily actions compounded over time into transformation. These tools moved me forward, but my anchor was always God. I remember one day vividly. I sat in my car outside the domestic violence courthouse, tears streaming silently down my face, my hands clenched on the steering wheel. I whispered through sobs, "God, I don't know how to end this nightmare, but I trust You'll show me the way." And He did. Not immediately, but slowly over time in lots of miraculous little ways. He did not rob me of the healing or growth process by instantly delivering me out. He planted me in. In the soil of hardship. In the slow, sacred process of healing. In the hidden place of inner restoration. It felt like I was buried. Forgotten. But God wasn't punishing me. He was planting me. I began to understand that the dirt wasn't a grave. It was a garden. I clung to the verse that God *"will give them beauty for ashes, and joy for mourning"* (Isaiah 61:3 *NKJV*).

In that dark place, something sacred began to take root. God wasn't looking for performance. This was welcome news to this overachiever. He was calling me to be present. While the world around me shifted, He invited me to anchor deeper in Him. Not in my roles or responsibilities. Not in others' opinions. Not even in my own strength. He reminded me that the true foundation of a thriving life isn't applause or approval. It's in abiding in Him.

I clung to Scripture like oxygen. I wrote declarations and taped them onto my mirror. I walked in nature, whispering prayers, asking God to remind me who I was, not based on my brokenness but on His promises. I declared, *"I am loved. I am a daughter of the King. I am growing every day. I lack nothing. I am beautiful. I am courageous and brave. I am given new mercies every day. I am meant to thrive. I* am strengthened in weakness. I am a joy to God. I am a warrior. I am a beacon of hope for others. I am highly favored. I am covered and shielded by God. I am not alone. I am cared for." Those hidden moments of truth and tears became sacred ground. God was deepening my roots. And He does that in the dark.

Just when I thought I had made it through the worst, God began to prune. He lovingly, but painfully, cut away the things I thought I needed. My people-pleasing, my fear of judgment, my need to hold it all together, my false sense of identity from being "the strong one," and my attachment to occupational titles. My priorities shifted from full-time mom to empty nester. I moved to a new state and began a new life. John 15:2 came alive to me: *"Every branch that does bear fruit He prunes, so that it will be even more fruitful."*

I wasn't being rejected. I was being refined. He cut away lies I had believed in myself. He severed relationships that no longer served my growth. He cleared out mindsets that kept me small and stuck. It hurt. But pruning always precedes purpose. God didn't just prune me, He watered me. He surrounded me with people of deep compassion and fierce faith, people who reminded me it was okay to not be okay. He gave me small wins, one good day, an unexpected smile from a stranger, a new opportunity that found me, a thankful word from my girls, one breakthrough moment at a time.

I began to show up for myself in ways I never had before. I started eating with intention, focusing on nutrition instead of emotional survival. I drank clean water throughout the day. I moved my body as an act of worship, honoring the strength God had given me. I spoke life over myself, my circumstances, to everyone within earshot.

Journaling prayers and gratitude became my way to count the miracles that showed up more each day. I was watering my garden.

Every habit was a seed. Every routine became a pathway forward into the joyful, purposeful, impactful, and blessed life I wanted. Each day became a step of redemption, redefining, and transformation into the woman God created me to be, a reflection of His grace and a beacon of hope for others still trapped in survival.

In time, God turned my survival into strength. He led me to serve again, but not from empty performance, instead from overflow. Service became my way out. I found a home in network marketing where my gifts of community building, equipping leaders, and creating a culture of heart-centered living were welcomed and wanted. I built a thriving global wellness and faith community filled with friends who are rising together.

Blooming Where I'm Planted

I began coaching women, leading retreats, writing books, and creating programs rooted in mindset, faith, and healing. I stopped asking, "Why me?" and began declaring, "Because me." I no longer asked, "When will it get better?" Instead, I began to proclaim, "It's already beginning." My health has shifted. My energy has risen. My faith deepened. My girls blossomed. My vision expanded. My passions grew. My breath became easier. I was no longer grasping for survival, I was now thriving with overflowing joy, vibrant wellness, meaningful relationships, and a calling that felt lighter and more expansive than I ever dreamed.

Today, I live between two beach homes and beautiful communities. One in Ortley Beach, New Jersey, and one in Delray Beach, Florida. These allow me to be close to my grandchildren and present for the people I love. I have a thriving online business and a faith-based wellness community I can serve from anywhere. My girls are all grown, most married, some moms themselves, and we are navigating deeper adult mother-daughter relationships. I get to watch them step into their lives, support them in building their dreams, and celebrate as they become the best versions of themselves. My business is flourishing. My heart is open. My relationships are richer. Opportunities chase me down, and I am grateful.

"This is the day the Lord has made. I will rejoice and be glad in it" (Psalm 118:24). He truly does make beauty from ashes, and your mess can become your message of hope. I used to pray with tears in my eyes and only hope in my heart. Now, I live it out loud with overflowing joy. Life is not always easy, even now, but I have learned to find peace and joy in the process. That allows me to show up in my life the way I want, regardless of circumstances. It allows me to create a life I love, a faith that strengthens me, a body that is healthy, a business that provides financial freedom, and a love that expands and impacts everyone it touches.

God uses the dirt. Do not despise your hard seasons. They are the soil of something sacred. You are not being buried, you are being planted. The darkness is not your end. It is your beginning. Pruning is not rejection. It is preparation for greater fruit. You were made to bloom, even here, especially now. Serve your way out. When you feel stuck, you sow seeds of love, kindness, and hope. They always return multiplied.

Victory Declaration

I am planted with divine purpose. I am not buried; I am becoming. God is restoring all that was lost, and I am blooming into my most joyful, impactful, faith-filled self. My life is a garden of grace, and I will thrive where I am planted.

A Blessing for You

Father, I thank You for the one reading these words. I pray that no matter what season they are in, they will know they are not buried but planted. Water their souls with Your peace. Strengthen their roots in Your love. Give them courage to take the next step, even if they cannot see the whole path. Heal the places that hurt. Restore their joy. And let their life become a testimony of Your goodness. In Jesus's name, Amen.

Reflections for You

- Where have you felt "buried" lately, and how might that actually be a planting?

- Which roots need strengthening right now, whether in the Word, prayer, worship, community, or service?

- What habits or identities might God be pruning so that new growth can come?

- Where are you still waiting for rescue instead of taking the next faithful step? What is that step?

- How can you "serve your way out" of confusion today, through one simple act of kindness or leadership?

- What signs of grace, whether small wins, unexpected help, or quiet peace, has God sent that you can celebrate today?

Connect with Tami:

ENLIGHTENMENT

What "THE GRASS GROWS WHERE I AM" Means to Me

> *A heartfelt reminder that my body was gifted with all it needs to heal, flourishing when I nurture it with love and care. Now that I've healed myself, I'm channeling that passion to help others heal, spreading hope and vitality to those around me.*

Dr. Samantha Carney

Connect with Dr. Sam:

What "THE GRASS GROWS WHERE I AM" Means to Me

> *The impact of presence and purposeful action—wherever I stand, I strive to foster growth, healing, and connection by creating a ripple effect of positive change wherever I am.*

Dr. Daniel Hulsey

Connect with Dr. Dan:

A Journey of Wisdom and Enlightenment: Biohacking Chiropractic Care

Dr. Daniel Hulsey & Dr. Samantha Carney

You can't fix structural issues with chemical solutions.
—Dr. Daniel Hulsey

My journey, and the shared vision that Dr. Samantha Carney and I forged, is anything but a conventional narrative. It's a story that stretches from the stark realities of combat zones to the nuanced and precise art of chiropractic care, ultimately leading to the establishment of Atlas Clinics in Pompano Beach, Florida. This clinic is more than just a practice; it's a testament to the power of personal experience, the limitations of conventional approaches, and the revolutionary potential of combining chiropractic principles with the cutting-edge advancements of biohacking.

My early life was deeply shaped by a profound sense of duty and a strong desire to serve. This innate drive led me to a career in the military, where I would be confronted with the raw, unfiltered realities of the human body under extreme duress. My time in

Afghanistan was not just a test of physical and mental endurance; it was a profound education in human anatomy, physiology, and the delicate interplay of systems that govern our health. I witnessed firsthand the incredible resilience of the human body. I saw its capacity to withstand tremendous stress and trauma, to endure injuries that would seem insurmountable, and to continue functioning even in the face of overwhelming adversity.

But I also witnessed its vulnerability. I learned about the delicate balance of systems, the intricate communication networks that allow us to move, feel, and heal. I saw how easily this balance could be disrupted by injury, how a single misstep or a moment of impact could have cascading effects throughout the entire organism. During my service, I sustained injuries that would profoundly impact on my life. These injuries weren't just superficial wounds; they affected the deeper structural integrity of my body, disrupting the intricate communication network that governs every aspect of our being.

The traditional medical system offered treatments, and I am grateful for the relief they provided from some of the immediate symptoms. However, I began to feel a growing dissatisfaction with the conventional approach. The medications and therapies, while helpful in managing pain and inflammation, often seemed like temporary solutions, like bandages on a deeper structural problem. They addressed the symptoms, but they didn't seem to address the underlying issues that were causing those symptoms. This dissatisfaction became a turning point. It sparked a fundamental question: Was there a more holistic approach to healing? Was there a way to address the root causes of these imbalances, to facilitate the body's own innate healing capabilities rather than simply suppressing its symptoms? This question led me to explore alternative and complementary therapies, approaches that focused on the body not as a collection of isolated parts but as an interconnected, dynamic system. It was during this exploration that I first encountered the principles of chiropractic care.

A Parallel Path: From Chronic Pain to Chiropractic

While my journey began on the battlefield, Dr. Samantha Carney's path to chiropractic was a personal one, born out of her own struggles with chronic pain and the limitations of conventional medical treatment. From a young age, she experienced frequent headaches, a constant companion that cast a shadow over her childhood and adolescence. These weren't just ordinary headaches; they were intense, debilitating, and seemingly inescapable.

When Samantha was sixteen, a traumatic event, a car accident, further exacerbated her condition. The accident resulted in a concussion, and despite her doctor's recommendations of rest and conventional therapies, her headaches and migraines worsened, becoming a daily struggle. This chronic pain was not just a physical affliction; it took a significant toll on her entire life. The constant pain affected her ability to concentrate, to focus, and to engage with the world around her. She went from being a straight-A student in high school, with a bright future and boundless potential, to failing classes in college, her academic aspirations derailed by the relentless pounding in her head. The pain was accompanied by a constellation of other symptoms: overwhelming anxiety, bouts of depression that seemed to come out of nowhere, and an uncontrollable weight gain that further eroded her self-esteem and sense of well-being.

Her health deteriorated, and she felt lost and hopeless, trapped in a cycle of pain and despair. In her desperation, Samantha turned to her mother, who suggested a path she had not yet considered: chiropractic care. Her mother had experienced the benefits of chiropractic firsthand and believed it could offer a solution where conventional medicine had failed. Working with her mother's chiropractor, Samantha began to experience something she had almost forgotten was possible: relief. The consistent adjustments gradually reduced the intensity and frequency of her headaches. It wasn't an overnight miracle, but a gradual, steady improvement that offered a glimmer of hope.

For the first time, she felt like her body was not her enemy but a system that could be helped, that could be brought back into balance. Impressed by the transformative power of chiropractic, Samantha decided to pursue a career in this field. This decision was not just about finding a profession; it was about a profound shift in perspective, a realization that there was a different way to approach health and healing. She applied to Palmer College of Chiropractic, Florida Campus, eager to learn the principles and techniques that had brought her so much relief. However, her journey was not without its challenges.

When she arrived at Palmer and began attending classes, the headaches, which had become more manageable, started to return. The stress of the academic environment, the long hours of studying, and the unfamiliar surroundings seemed to trigger the old patterns of pain. She sought adjustments at the student clinic, but the care provided by students still learning their craft did not provide the same level of relief she had experienced with her previous chiropractor. This was a frustrating setback, a reminder of the fragility of her progress and the need for a more refined and effective approach.

The Convergence of Paths
A Shared Vision Takes Root

It was at Palmer College that our paths converged. I was driven by my own dissatisfaction with conventional medicine and my growing interest in holistic healing, and had arrived at Palmer College seeking to deepen my knowledge and refine my skills. My military experience had instilled in me a deep respect for the body's resilience but also a profound awareness of its limitations when its structural integrity was compromised. I was drawn to chiropractic because its principles resonated deeply with my intuitive understanding of the body. I saw it, not as a collection of isolated parts, but as a complex, integrated whole where the structure of the spine played a crucial role in overall health and function.

And Samantha, with her firsthand experience of the transformative power of chiropractic, brought a unique perspective to her studies. She understood the limitations of treating symptoms and the importance of addressing the root causes of pain and dysfunction. She had felt the difference between temporary relief and true healing, and she was determined to learn how to provide that kind of lasting change for others. Samantha expressed her frustration about her persistent headaches to me. She described the challenges she was facing, the return of the pain, and the difficulty in finding effective relief within the college clinic. I listened empathetically, recognizing the familiar struggle of seeking genuine healing in a system that often prioritized standardized protocols over individualized care.

I shared my own experiences with the limitations of traditional approaches and how I had found true healing by addressing the root cause of my issues. I told her about a particular type of chiropractic care that had changed my life, a technique that went beyond simply manipulating the spine to address the deeper neurological and biomechanical imbalances that often underline chronic pain. I urged her to trust me and allow me to guide her toward this solution. I knew, from my own experience, that it could offer the relief she was seeking, the lasting change she desperately needed. I made an appointment for her and drove her to the clinic where I had received this life-changing care.

There, Samantha underwent a comprehensive examination that went far beyond the typical chiropractic assessment. The practitioner didn't just look at her spine; they evaluated her entire musculoskeletal system, her neurological function, and her overall posture and movement patterns. This thorough evaluation revealed the root of her problems: misalignments in her neck, particularly in the upper cervical spine. She received a specific adjustment, delivered with a precision and gentleness that was unlike anything she had experienced before. The technique involved the use of sound-wave technology, a noninvasive method that targeted the misalignments with remarkable accuracy. The following morning, Samantha woke up feeling like a different person. The brain fog that had clouded her mind for years had lifted. Her head was clear, and she was free from the constant grip of headaches.

What was even more remarkable was that this wasn't a temporary fix. The single adjustment provided relief that lasted for months. It wasn't just a masking of the symptoms but a genuine correction of the underlying problem. Suddenly, school became easier. Her grades improved, and she felt like her brain had finally turned on. The headaches were gone, her body felt lighter and more energetic, and she even began to lose weight, a side effect of the improved hormonal balance that often accompanies proper spinal alignment. Her menstrual cycles, which had been a source of pain and discomfort, became more manageable. Almost every aspect of her being had been positively transformed by this single sound-wave adjustment.

This experience was a revelation for Samantha. It shattered her preconceptions about chiropractic care and opened her eyes to the limitations of the traditional models she had been learning in school. She realized that there was a level of precision, a depth of understanding, and a potential for healing that went far beyond what she had been taught. She knew she could not, in good conscience, treat her future patients with anything less than the most effective and transformative care.

I, having experienced my own healing journey and witnessed Samantha's dramatic transformation, understood her conviction. My military training had instilled in me a mindset of continuous improvement, a desire to push beyond conventional limits and seek out the most effective solutions. We both began to question whether the healing process could be further optimized. Was there a way to enhance the precision of chiropractic care, to make it even more targeted and effective? This question led us to explore the world of biohacking.

Embracing Biohacking
The Future of Chiropractic

Biohacking, the practice of using science and technology to optimize human biology, offered a new framework for us. It was a way of thinking about health and healing that resonated deeply with both of our experiences. We saw the potential to combine the fundamental principles of chiropractic with cutting-edge advancements in technology, nutrition, and lifestyle optimization to achieve even greater levels of healing and well-being. This wasn't about abandoning the core principles of chiropractic but about enhancing them, about using the tools of modern science to refine our understanding of the body and improve the precision and effectiveness of our interventions.

We began to explore the research on neurology, biomechanics, and cellular health, looking for ways to integrate these findings into our practice. I was particularly drawn to the EPIC technique, a comprehensive system that aligned with my growing understanding of the body's complex biomechanics and neurological pathways. This technique went beyond traditional spinal manipulation to address the deeper structural and functional imbalances that often underline chronic pain and dysfunction.

I experienced firsthand the power of EPIC. I witnessed the resolution of chronic headaches that had plagued patients for years, the silencing of persistent tinnitus that had disrupted their lives, the alleviation of debilitating TMJ pain that had made eating and speaking a daily struggle, and the fading of my own back pain, a constant reminder of my time in service. These weren't just isolated improvements; they were tangible manifestations of the body's remarkable ability to heal when provided with the right stimulus.

This personal validation fueled my conviction in the power of personalized, precision-based interventions, a cornerstone of biohacking. It reinforced the idea that each patient was unique, with a distinct set of needs and a specific set of imbalances that required a tailored approach. It wasn't enough to simply apply a standardized protocol; we needed to understand the individual's unique biology and address their specific needs with precision and accuracy.

During our time at Palmer College, Samantha and I found a shared passion for chiropractic and a commitment to patient-centered care. We were both dedicated to moving beyond standardized protocols and embracing individualized treatments, recognizing that each patient was unique with a distinct biological signature and a specific set of needs. This approach was a direct application of the biohacking ethos.

We saw firsthand the transformative results of this approach. Patients experienced significant improvements in their health and well-being that went far beyond what we had seen with traditional chiropractic care. Their pain decreased, their function improved, their energy levels increased, and their overall quality of life was enhanced. And the clinic's patient numbers grew steadily, a testament to the effectiveness of this new approach. These positive outcomes weren't just metrics of success; they were confirmations of the efficacy of this enlightened approach. It was a testament to the fact that when the body's individual needs are addressed with precision and a holistic understanding, the results can be truly remarkable.

From Education to Practice
The Birth of Atlas Clinics

After our time at Palmer, I sought further refinement of my skills at the EPIC Clinics Headquarters office. This immersion provided an invaluable opportunity to delve deeper into the intricacies of the technique, to learn from experienced practitioners who had mastered its nuances, and to hone my diagnostic and adjustment abilities. This period of focused learning further illuminated the interconnectedness of the body's systems. I witnessed firsthand how lifestyle factors, such as nutrition, stress management, and exercise, could significantly impact the effectiveness of chiropractic interventions. It became clear that true optimization, the essence of biohacking for chiropractic, required addressing the multifaceted nature of human health. It wasn't just about the spine; it was about the entire ecosystem of the individual.

The culmination of our journey was the establishment of Atlas Clinics in Pompano Beach. This clinic became the platform to implement our evolved philosophies of care, combining our unique backgrounds and shared vision. We wanted to create a space where patients could experience the full potential of chiropractic care, where they could receive personalized, precision-based treatment that addressed the root causes of their health challenges and empowered them to achieve optimal well-being. At Atlas Clinics, we moved beyond the limitations of traditional approaches, embracing the principles of biohacking and a deep respect for the body's innate healing capabilities. We assembled a team of like-minded practitioners who shared our commitment to excellence, innovation, and patient-centered care. We invested in cutting edge technology, sought out the latest research, and continuously refined our techniques to ensure that we were providing the most effective and advanced care possible.

The Atlas Soundwave Revolution
A New Era of Precision

The introduction of the ATLAS Soundwave technique represents the culmination of our journey. This technology is more than just an advancement; it is a manifestation of the enlightenment we have gained regarding the critical role of the atlas vertebra in overall health. The atlas vertebra, the topmost bone in the spine, is a unique and crucial junction. It's where the skull meets the spine, and it plays a vital role in supporting the head, protecting the brainstem, and facilitating the flow of neurological information between the brain and the body. We understand that this crucial junction is not simply a structural component but a vital gateway for neurological communication.

Even minute misalignments in this area can have cascading effects throughout the entire body. They can disrupt nerve flow, interfere with the brain's ability to communicate with the body's organs and tissues, and hinder the body's self-healing mechanisms. These misalignments, often subtle and undetected by conventional diagnostic methods, can contribute to a wide range of health problems, from headaches and neck pain to digestive issues, hormonal imbalances, and compromised immune function.

The precision of the ATLAS Soundwave allows for targeted correction of these subtle misalignments. Unlike traditional chiropractic adjustments, which often involve manual manipulation and forceful movements, the ATLAS Soundwave utilizes gentle yet powerful sound waves to restore proper alignment. This approach embodies the core tenets of biohacking for chiropractic: leveraging advanced technology to deliver precise interventions that optimize the body's inherent function with minimal invasiveness. It recognizes the body's sensitivity and seeks to work in harmony with its natural healing processes. The sound waves gently resonate with the tissues of the atlas vertebra, stimulating the body's own healing mechanisms to restore alignment and improve neurological function. This technique is not only more precise than traditional adjustments, but it is also more comfortable and less likely to cause discomfort or injury. The enlightenment gained through this journey extends beyond the technical aspects of chiropractic care.

We understand that true healing isn't just about the absence of pain or the correction of structural imbalances. It's about fostering a state of optimal well-being, where the body and mind are functioning in harmony, where the individual can thrive on all levels. This holistic perspective informs every aspect of our practice at Atlas Clinics, from the initial consultation to the ongoing care plan. We take the time to listen to our patients, to understand their individual needs and goals, and to develop a personalized treatment plan that addresses the root causes of their health challenges. We also educate our patients about the importance of lifestyle factors, such as nutrition, exercise, and stress management, and how these factors can impact their overall health and well-being.

At Atlas Clinics, we have created an environment where healing and optimization are the guiding principles. Our combined enlightenment, gained through diverse experiences and a relentless pursuit of knowledge, has led to a practice that embraces the cutting edge of chiropractic care through the lens of biohacking. We are committed to providing our patients with the most advanced, effective, and personalized care possible. We understand that the human body possesses an inherent potential for growth, vitality, and resilience. By providing the right environment—precise adjustments, targeted interventions, and a holistic approach to well-being—we empower our patients to flourish, to overcome limitations, and to cultivate a life of optimal health and vitality. The enlightenment we have gained is not just our own; it is shared with each patient who walks through the doors of Atlas Clinics, embarking on their own journey of biohacked healing and a deeper understanding of their own remarkable potential.

> *If you listen to your body when it whispers,*
> *you don't have to hear it when it screams.*
> —ANONYMOUS

Reflections for You

- What specific injury or health challenge from your past might be a "symptom" rather than the root cause, and how could exploring the body's interconnected systems (like the spine's role in nerve flow) change your approach to healing it?

- In what ways have you relied on symptom-masking treatments (e.g., painkillers), and what questions could you ask a healthcare provider to shift toward addressing underlying structural or neurological imbalances?

- Pick one daily thing (e.g., drinking more water, walking 10 minutes, or eating protein at breakfast) to support your spine and nerves—try it for three days and note how you feel.

- Perform a simple self-check: Gently assess your head posture over your shoulders in a mirror. Is your head directly over your shoulders or leaning forward? A small tilt here (the "atlas" area) can cause headaches, tiredness, or even dysfunction throughout the entire musculoskeletal system.

- If a friend has endless migraines or chronic pain, suggest they look for a chiropractor who uses precise tools (like gentle sound waves instead of hard twists) to fix the neck without force.

- Try a basic biohacking exercise: For 5 minutes daily, focus on deep breathing while visualizing clear communication between your brain and body via the spine. Reflect afterward on any shifts in energy, clarity, or pain levels.

Connect with Dr. Sam:
Connect with Dr. Dan:

What "THE GRASS GROWS WHERE I AM" Means to Me

> We need to look inside to find relief and release, and look deeper and around us to find our light fragmented and frozen due to Trauma, which other approaches can miss or suppress.
>
> Find the hidden seeds and with Full Self Recovery let's cultivate 'whole humans being' and together help the world Lighten UP.

Clive Digby-Jones

Connect with Clive:

The Art of Cultivating a Whole Human—the Missing Peace

Clive Digby-Jones

> *It is our job to find, integrate or reintegrate, fully embody and then fully radiate The Light, so that we (also light in form) and The Source Light can experience what it means to be fully human.*
>
> —Dr. Eileen Watkins Seymour DSc HC

The human condition, as I have come to observe over decades of immersion in the intricate landscapes of the psyche, is often characterized by a subtle, yet pervasive, undercurrent of unease. A vast majority of people, seemingly navigating the currents of daily life, are nonetheless subtly, or sometimes profoundly, burdened by negative emotional states. These undercurrents, like unseen eddies in a flowing stream, frequently manifest as discord, not only within the individual, but also rippling outward to disrupt the harmony of the world around them. This persistent observation has fueled a lifelong inquiry: What fundamental shifts are required to cultivate truly Whole Human Beings, people who radiate an inner peace that naturally contributes to a more peaceful planet? The insights offered by clinical psychologists, particularly those embracing a psycho-spiritual integration approach, resonate deeply with this quest. They speak of enlightenment, not as some lofty, unattainable ideal, but as a natural consequence of bringing together the fragmented aspects of our being. This integration, the very cornerstone of this exploration, promises a path toward a more complete and harmonious existence.

In my poem "Dancing in the Middle," I offer a lyrical invitation to consider our relationship with life itself. Are we participants, fully engaged in the vibrant center of experience, or are we relegated to the periphery, observing from a distance, perhaps shrouded by the "mists of emotional poverty"?

Do you dance in the middle or on the edge of life? Are your eyes open and filled with love? Or closed by the mists of emotional poverty?

Do you dance in the middle or on the edge of life? Can you touch the petals and feel the satin of a buttercup? Can you smell the dusky bark of ancient oak?

Do you dance in the middle or on the edge of life? As the child embraces the sky, can you reach for your destiny? And leap for joy and feel a teardrop dry?

Do you dance in the middle or on the edge of life? When you can hear the snowflake fall and create an anthem from the rain, when you look into the eyes of a child and your souls touch, then you are in the dance.

But when you are truly in love with yourself, your lover, and nature, then you are dancing in the middle, not on the edge of life.

The vibrant "dancing in the middle," arises from a profound and integrated love—for oneself, for one's intimate partner, and for the encompassing embrace of nature. This holistic connection forms the bedrock of a life lived fully, not tentatively from the sidelines. It encapsulates the full spectrum of human emotion, experienced and integrated rather than suppressed or avoided.

Having "danced the dance" myself, I endeavor to speak with the authority of lived experience. I strive to paint a picture of profound presence, where one can "hear the snowflake fall" and find music in the rhythm of the rain. The ultimate connection, however, lies in the deep resonance between souls, the unspoken understanding that passes between the eyes of a child.

My Journey

My own journey into understanding and facilitating this "dancing in the middle" has been deeply intertwined with the groundbreaking work of my life partner, Dr. Eileen Watkins Seymour, DSc HC. Eileen was a pioneer, introducing neuro linguistic programming (NLP) to Europe in the early 1980s and establishing the first diploma program in the prestigious London Business School. I had the privilege of participating in her final program in 1987–88 before she entrusted its continuation to her students.

NLP, at its core, illuminates the subjective nature of human experience. Imagine six people witnessing the same traffic accident. Each will offer a distinct account, not necessarily due to deliberate fabrication, but because each person processes the world through their unique sensory filters, affected by an inner energetic holding pattern. We each prioritize different aspects—what we see, hear, feel—and then interpret and describe these experiences in ways that reinforce our internal programming. This fundamental insight reveals a powerful truth: By shifting our inner programming (releasing withheld energy), we can fundamentally alter our perception and experience of the world.

Our collaborative exploration extended beyond the initial framework of NLP. Through Eileen's extensive work with psychotherapy clients, a deeper layer of understanding emerged. She observed a pattern of fragmentation, a subtle or sometimes significant withdrawal of our subtle energy in response to life's challenges. This observation led to the development of Wholistic NLP, a more profound approach that addressed not just cognitive patterns but also the energetic architecture of the self. I vividly recall a moment that encapsulates the innovative spirit of Eileen's work. At the launch of Stephen Hawking's seminal book, *A Brief History of Time*, Eileen found herself in conversation with the legendary physicist, describing my article on "Black Holes in the Internal Universe." This concept, born from our observations of fragmented energy within the psyche, resonated with the profound mysteries Hawking explored in the cosmos. Our ideas continued to evolve. An article I penned on Wholistic NLP for a new UK journal on the subject garnered an invitation to present our work in California. There, our approach, which had taken root at the Ravenscroft Centre we established in Golders Green, London, became known as the Ravenscroft Approach.

As we embarked on the design of our practitioner training program around the year 2000, we sought accreditation from CPCAB (the Counselling and Psychotherapy Central Awarding Body). The examiner, who had previously organized workshops for us both in the UK and on the idyllic island of Crete, recognized the unique nature of our work. He astutely observed that our training transcended existing categories, necessitating the creation of a new classification: "psycho-spiritual integration." Thus, the Ravenscroft Approach to psycho-spiritual integration was formally recognized, and our book, *The Missing Peace: The Advanced Seeker's Guide to Wholeness*, was published in the UK in 2003, articulating the core principles of this transformative approach. The affirmation from clinical psychologists, highlighting psycho-spiritual integration as a pathway to enlightenment, further solidified its significance.

Our journey together, spanning over three decades in this lifetime and, we believe, echoing across others, has been one of shared exploration and mutual growth. Drawing upon my own experiences as a top graduate of Dale Carnegie courses, I learned the importance of earning the right to speak on a subject. While Eileen often prefers to focus on the direct work of healing and transformation, I, as her student, former client, and life partner, feel a deep responsibility and privilege to share this breakthrough approach with you. To illustrate its profound impact, I will often draw upon the example of releasing grief, a deeply entrenched and often debilitating emotion that affects so many.

In a playful yet profound way, I once captured the essence of this work in a poem, "Putting Humpty Dumpty (Clive Digby-Jones) Together Again," inspired by the familiar nursery rhyme. Queen RAPSI®, a symbolic representation of the Ravenscroft Approach to Psycho-Spiritual Integration, embodies the gentle yet powerful process of restoring wholeness.

> *All the king's horses and all the king's men couldn't put Clive together again!*
>
> *The king was distraught, Queen RAPSI® was not! She gathered the pieces unheeded. "And although there's a mess, I can see deep inside that it's light that's desperately needed."*
>
> *She helped him explore as Clive awoke, and the hurt and the cracks receded. The magic was working, light shone all around. Once again, Queen RAPSI® succeeded.*

Higher Consciousness

Through our work, Eileen and I have come to understand that many belief systems and healing practices often focus on the commendable goal of raising one's vibration and connecting with higher energy. However, the Ravenscroft Approach introduces a crucial distinction: the importance of identifying and recovering our own "missing energy." This energy, often fragmented and withdrawn as a protective mechanism in response to traumatic life experiences, both in this lifetime and potentially others, needs to be actively retrieved and reintegrated.

Simply focusing on managing or neutralizing symptoms, while sometimes necessary, may not address the underlying energetic fragmentation. You may have encountered the notion that we are inherently whole and perfect, and that our journey is simply one of reuniting with our creator. While there is a profound truth in our inherent divine spark, our experience suggests that our energy can indeed become fragmented. The path to wholeness involves not just remembering our connection to the divine, but also actively recovering, embodying, and then radiating all aspects of our own unique energy. This process transforms us into what we call a "Light Vehicle," capable of receiving and integrating higher and other dimensional energies, which in turn triggers the Quantum Law of Attraction, drawing to us the people, resources, and opportunities necessary for our own healing and the healing of others.

As Eileen eloquently stated in *The Missing Peace*: *"It is our job to find, integrate or reintegrate, fully embody, and then fully radiate The Light, so that we and The Source Light can experience what it means to be fully human."*

Once we learn to harness and radiate our own inherent light, we become capable of drawing in deeper levels of higher consciousness, effectively "fertilizing our buried seeds" of potential. It is in these moments of energetic integration that profound clarity and genuine enlightenment arise. This journey of personal development unfolds through four distinct stages, a pattern we have observed consistently in our work with clients:

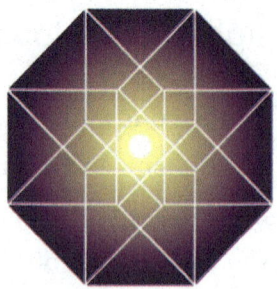

The Missing Peace—The symbol for the 5th Dimension. Wholeness

- **STAGE ONE: Sleepwalking through your existence.** This stage is characterized by a primary focus on survival—securing basic needs such as food and shelter for oneself and one's family. Life is often experienced as a series of tasks and responsibilities, leaving little time for introspection or reflection. People in this stage are often deeply immersed in the demands of the external world, making it challenging to engage with inner work, even something as simple as reading a book or this chapter. There may be an inclination to control or suppress uncomfortable symptoms, both physical and emotional. Does this resonate with your current experience?

- **STAGE TWO: Becoming self-aware.** This marks a significant awakening. Individuals in this stage begin to recognize a sense of less than, a feeling that despite external achievements, something fundamental is missing. They may start to reflect on their past, perhaps examining childhood experiences and noticing patterns of unmet needs or painful events. A search for deeper meaning and understanding often begins, perhaps leading them to resources like this book. This stage involves the nascent discovery of an inner world, a realm of thoughts, feelings, and perhaps a dawning awareness of an inner or spiritual self. Does this describe a shift you are currently undergoing?

- **STAGE THREE: Managing yourself.** This stage builds upon self-awareness, focusing on acquiring tools and techniques for self-discovery and the management of one's reactions, feelings, interactions, and daily life. People may join groups, study various self-help methodologies, follow teachers or coaches, and even develop their own personal practices and rituals. Experiences of raising one's vibration, and even exploring altered states of consciousness, may become part of their journey. There is often a desire to share this newfound knowledge with others. While this stage represents significant progress, we have observed a potential limitation: One or more parts of the self may still be in a position of managing the rest, even when there is a conscious intention to surrender to a higher power. The ego is often mistakenly blamed for these internal dynamics. Furthermore, our clinical observations have revealed that while techniques aimed at understanding or neutralizing symptoms like fear, anxiety, depression, pain, and grief can provide temporary relief and even overlay positive feelings, they may inadvertently leave the underlying "frozen missing energy" unaddressed. One participant in our study poignantly described this as the "rubber band effect": *"I had spent 50 years using various methods to rise above, go beyond and install a better memory, but you helped me find and release the nagging pin prick in my chest, which was like a rubber band anchored in the past, where I stretched forward in my life achieving greatness, until I could go no further."* Does this resonate with any aspect of your own journey?

- **STAGE FOUR: Self-actualization.** For us, this is not simply about achieving one's potential in the external world but rather the profound process of becoming whole. It involves actively finding, embodying, and radiating our missing source of light energy, leading to a deep sense of inner knowing. I personally experience this as becoming a "Light Vehicle"—like an old car that has been fully repaired, with all its parts functioning optimally. No longer burdened by missing components, this vehicle is now free to travel, explore, and receive greater awareness, unhindered by internal deficits. Higher and more expansive energies and learnings can now be fully integrated. A crucial initial step in this stage is honest self-inquiry: Are there parts of you that are still managing other parts? Have you perhaps unconsciously masked underlying missing aspects of yourself? While our physical bodies have a finite lifespan and may show signs of wear and tear, the potential for inner wholeness and profound experience remains. Are you perhaps already a "driving instructor" for others on their path? Does this resonate with your current aspirations?

Four Orders of Reality

To further understand this journey toward wholeness, it is helpful to consider the **Four Orders of Reality**. As beings often primarily identified with our physical bodies, we tend to be most consciously aware of the last two orders. However, cultivating awareness of the first two is essential for profound psycho-spiritual integration:

1. **Essence/Source Light:** This is the deepest, innermost sense of self, the core of our being. Accessible through practices like meditation, source light represents a powerful and fundamental driving force within us, the vitality of which can fluctuate throughout our lives.

2. **Energetic Holding Patterns:** These are the imprints of past experiences, where fragmented energy becomes withheld, often manifesting as inner child selves or inner others (representations of significant figures from our past, including family and even ancestral influences). These are more than mere memories; they

can become frozen pockets of energy within us or even be expelled from our energetic field.

3. **Body World:** This encompasses our physical form, its functioning, and the physical, emotional, and mental symptoms we experience throughout our lives. These symptoms are often the surface manifestations of deeper energetic imbalances.

4. **The Outside World:** This is the external environment and our conscious responses to it. Our interactions with the world are significantly shaped by the underlying energetic and emotional landscape within us.

Finally, to truly grasp the journey of becoming whole, we must consider the unfolding of our "light" as it takes form and interacts with the world. As I once read and adapted: *"Tell me everything, I'm listening. Give me your language for each of your pains, your unending griefs, your tired aches. Show me your wounds and let them breathe. Allow your heart to crack wide open as you sift through its broken walls to see what still fits and if new pieces have been made. Let us help you find the pieces, recover your light, your missing self, and radiate a whole peace."*

Recovering Our Missing Self

The journey toward recovering our missing self often begins with a process of honest self-inquiry, guided by three fundamental steps:

Step 1. How much of your energy is missing?

This question invites a deep, intuitive response from your entire system rather than a purely cognitive calculation. On a scale of 1 to 10, where 10 represents being fully present in every moment—in your physical presence, your touch, your relationships—how close to a 10 would you say you are on average? Consider the examples of clients we have worked with: a man who had lived with clinical depression for fifty years assessed his "NOW Score" at a 2 out of 10, despite significant external achievements. Another client, feeling stuck and unproductive, placed herself at 5 out of 10, experiencing an internal conflict of opposing forces. Rarely do individuals assess themselves above 8, indicating that even in seemingly high-functioning individuals, approximately 20 percent or more of their potential energetic presence may be unavailable. In a more extreme case, a client in Los Angeles grappling with Crohn's disease and a profound loss of faith assessed his NOW Score at a –2, indicating a significant depletion of his vital energy. The common thread in these diverse experiences is the recognition that a substantial portion of their energy—80 percent, 50 percent, even a staggering 120 percent in the last example—was yet to be found and integrated. Take a moment now to ask yourself: **What is my NOW Score?** Allow your intuition, your gut feeling, to guide your response. Your conscious mind may attempt to rationalize or overestimate, so trust the more subtle signals from your inner being. If your mind confidently declares you a 10, perhaps consider asking a trusted partner or child for their perspective on your average level of presence with them. Their feedback can offer valuable insights.

Step 2. Where is the missing percentage?

Having gained a sense of the extent of missing energy, the next step involves identifying the doorways through which this energy may have been lost or fragmented. These doorways often manifest as pain points, physical symptoms, or recurring emotional patterns.

Lara's story is a profound example of how trauma fragments our subtle energy, freezing it at a younger age and creating "struggle patterns" that manifest as physical illness. After years of stomach issues and bloodwork suggesting possible cancer, Lara refused traditional medication and instead attended six sessions with Eileen, which I observed.

In the first two sessions, Eileen helped Lara define her present state. She identified her patterns (controlling, hiding, etc.) and negative feelings (fear, anxiety) as "headlines" with minimal background. She then defined her desired outcomes: feeling confident, relaxed, pain-free, and recognized. Lara was asked to provide a "presence score" on a scale of 1 to 10, with 10 representing being fully present. She rated herself a 6/10, meaning 60% of her energy was present while 40% was "missing." She then visualized a "10 out of 10" future self, detailing how that version of her would look and behave. Using an intuitive scoreboard, she graded her present self against these desired elements; some areas scored a 6 or 7, while others were as low as 2. These internal personas were labeled "Present Self" and "Future Self." Interestingly, the Future Self later confirmed it had been "out front" all along, waiting to be integrated into the body to bring a sense of wholeness.

Lara's homework was to visualize her Present and Future Selves getting to know each other and to take notes on memories and realizations throughout the week. We used the "birdies in the nest" metaphor: as you feed one starving bird (an aspect of self), the next one appears. As positive feelings increase, it is vital not to lose faith when the next "frozen" energy emerges; it is all part of a building process. We began the deep work by having Lara visualize her 60% present energy in one hand and her 40% missing energy in the other. We traced the "missing" 40% back to its origin: Age 4. Lara visualized her four-year-old self and identified which hand held that younger energy. She explored the masculine and feminine energies of that time, recalling who had hurt or denied her.

Lara created a safe place in nature for her four-year-old self and introduced her to the Present and Future Selves. Together, these three versions of Lara identified the "inner others"—parents, teachers, and abusers—who had caused her trauma. She visualized a "holding room" or stadium where these figures were seated comfortably with refreshments. Her Present Self then locked the door, freeing the system to work with her younger selves one at a time. In Lara's case, age 4 was a pivotal fragment that had been unconsciously running her adult thoughts and actions. This younger self helped her find a "doorway" in her stomach that led back to the womb, revealing a need for healing between the birth mother and the fetus. This work resulted in the birth of a "fully lit" newborn. As the baby's light became part of age 4, Lara felt a massive release of frozen energy, accompanied by deep sobbing and relief.

This sparked a "relay race" of healing. As each age-specific fragment spoke its truth, the "inner others" were healed or reconciled. Lara's energy, which had been mixed with her abusers' energy as a protective or punitive measure, was reclaimed. As these "inner others" were released, Lara experienced physical sensations of tingling, warmth, and calmness. Each dissolved fragment added to her "energy stash," updating her system age by age. By the third session, Lara discovered a fourteen-year-old fragment standing behind her—a defensive, untrusting energy that was "tripping her up" in life. In the fourth session, Lara used "x-ray vision" to see through the protective layers of this fourteen-year-old: darkness, brown, red, and yellow.

Once Lara acknowledged these layers as protectors, they identified the feelings they were guarding: fear, false safety, anger, and loneliness. As these layers dissolved, the pure "source light" of her fourteen-year-old self flooded her body through her lower back and stomach. This light expanded beyond her skin, filling the room and the neighborhood, acting as a "quantum law of attraction" to magnetize what she needed. In her final sessions, Lara's presence score rose steadily to 10/10. She predicted that her stomach symptoms would vanish within six weeks. Indeed, six weeks after her final session, Lara's blood tests were completely clear. She had become fully herself and eventually went on to become a therapist. Lara's journey highlights the importance of identifying frozen fragments and recovering the "Missing Peace" to live a rejuvenated life.

What fragments of your energy are frozen in or around you? What symptoms do these fragments produce? How might recovering your Missing Peace improve your life?

Step 3. Embarking on an inner journey.

Working with a trained practitioner of psycho-spiritual integration facilitates a guided inner journey to locate the specific frozen energetic structures associated with past experiences. Through gentle guidance, individuals are supported in sensing and "seeing in" to these areas and then helped to release and embody the previously missing energy. This process often brings immediate relief, a sense of lightness, and an expansion of one's overall being.

The Ravenscroft Approach utilizes a framework known as the **5 R's: Recognition, Relationship, Reconciliation, Release,** and **Radiating.** This iterative process allows for gradual and compassionate engagement with the past. If you are a psychologist, healer, therapist, coach, or social worker, let us help you add psycho-spiritual integration to your toolkit. We are seeking centers of excellence to include RAPSI®, the Ravenscroft Approach to psycho-spiritual integration.

Reflections for You

- What daily routines have you been using to stay centered, create joy and love, and be present?

- Do you "dance" in the middle or on the edge of life? Do you feel a sense of groundedness, wholeness, all the time? If not, what percentage of you—your energy/light—might still be withheld like a rubber band anchored in the past?

- Are you yet a "Light Vehicle," fully embodying the "higher energies" and radiating, triggering the quantum law of attraction?

- If 10/10 is being fully present, on average, how much of you is there still to find, reconnect, and integrate? To Be or Fully Be, that is the question!

- Are you helping others find their full Source Light? To become a Light Vehicle?

What "THE GRASS GROWS WHERE I AM" Means to Me

> Life's gonna life, but I'm the one that gets to say how it's gonna go—happy, messy, calm, or wild. So why's the grass greener here? Simple. I'm here. And when I say it's green… it is.

Ricki Moskow

Connect with Ricki:

Name It, Frame It & Claim It

Ricki Moskow

*Happiness isn't something we wait for.
It's something we create, even in the middle of the mess.*

My name is Ricki Moskow, but I now resonate with *RADOSH*. Radosh means joy in Polish. I'm not actually changing my legal name, but I use it on social media and when I speak because it's a powerful reminder for me, and for anyone listening, that joy is a choice. I've adopted Radosh as a pen name, a brand name for a new way of living. It's a banner under which I share my story and my philosophy. This isn't the fluffy, performative kind of joy you see everywhere. It's the real kind. The kind that shows up in the thick of it when things are hard, messy, and uncertain. It's the joy you must build for yourself, brick by brick, belief by belief. My life is amazing. Truly. And it's not amazing because everything worked out perfectly or because I was handed a stress-free path. It's amazing because I made it that way. I chose to be happy. I built joy into my life with one breath, one decision, one inner conversation at a time. And when I wasn't happy, I didn't wait for something to change, I changed the way I met the moment. This wasn't just a decision; it was a slow, deliberate movement toward enlightenment, a conscious awakening to my own power.

It wasn't always like this. I spent most of my life in the background. I've always been someone who smiled easily, stayed calm when others couldn't, and kept things together without making a fuss. People would describe me as grounded, steady, and reliable. That was true but it wasn't the full picture. What they didn't see was how often I played small. I stayed quiet. I watched and observed and waited. I told myself it was safer to be invisible, like I had this silent deal with the world: Don't look at me and I won't look at you. I believed if I didn't draw attention to myself, I couldn't be criticized, judged, or hurt. Hiding felt like a form of protection. I convinced myself that my inner world was too fragile for public scrutiny, so I pretended to be a simple, unremarkable person to keep the world at a safe distance.

I remember my ten-year high school reunion like it was yesterday. The room was a cacophony of loud laughter and clinking glasses, a swirling current of people catching up on what they had become. I chose a seat in the back, a familiar spot at a small, round table. I was an observer, just as I had been in the hallways of our school, watching everyone else live out the movie of their lives. A woman I vaguely remembered from my chemistry class came over to me. Her smile was wide, but her eyes held a spark of knowing and perhaps a touch of pity. "Some things never change, Ricki," she said, her voice a little too loud over the music. When I asked what she meant, a familiar lump formed in my throat as she gestured with her chin toward the room. *"This is exactly how you were in high school, just sitting and watching everyone else."*

She wasn't wrong. Her words weren't malicious, but they landed with the force of a truth I had been running from my entire life. It wasn't an accusation; it was a mirror. And in that reflection, I saw not the happy, grounded person everyone thought I was but a ghost of a person who was present but not participating. The moment stirred something in me, a deep discomfort that I could no longer ignore. I started noticing a pattern. I'd join a group, maybe twenty or thirty people in a circle. I'd tell myself, "Just sit back, don't say anything, just listen." And somehow, I'd end up in the middle of the circle, speaking. Again, and again.

That's when it hit me: If I was trying so hard to disappear, why did I keep stepping into the center? I wasn't invisible. I was pretending to be. The pretense was a habit, a comfortable old coat I wore to feel safe. But it was a coat that was suffocating me. The pattern I noticed was my quiet gravitation to the center of the room. It was my authentic self pushing back against the role I had assigned myself. My deep self knew I had a voice, knew I had something to offer. It was a silent rebellion against my own self-imposed invisibility.

A Leader

What I finally saw is that I've always been a leader. Not the loudest voice in the room, but the one people came to for steadiness. I wanted people to feel good, to feel connected. I noticed the dynamics. I quietly held space. I created environments where people felt safe and seen. And I was the one they learned from. The moment I realized I wasn't in the background and that I had just been hiding there was the beginning of everything. Because that's when I knew I had something to offer. It was a small but profound moment of enlightenment, a flash of self-awareness that changed everything.

The world didn't need me to shrink; it needed me to be fully present. The clarity it brought was like a fog lifted from around me. I saw my entire past through a new lens: not as a story of a quiet, shy person, but as a story of someone who was always a leader, a guiding force who just hadn't claimed her role. That simple shift in perspective made my entire life make sense. It gave me permission to stop pretending, to stop playing small, and to finally step into the full power of who I truly am. That's also when I saw the truth: Life doesn't care about your plans. It throws what it throws. I could either spend my time complaining about what wasn't working, or I could decide to see what was happening and make the best of it.

Over time, I found myself doing something very simple, repeatedly, whenever things felt off or heavy or uncertain. It was in these moments that I learned to build true resilience, not by avoiding the storm, but by learning to navigate it with a steady hand. This wasn't a skill I learned from a book; it was a muscle I developed by showing up for myself, again. I didn't set out to create a process, but I ended up with one. The process wasn't born out of a strategic plan; it was forged in the fire of countless quiet moments where I had to face my own discomfort and uncertainty. If you had met me years ago, you might have seen me as the one in the background. I let other people take center stage while I handled everything quietly organizing, smoothing things over, making sure things happened.

But here's the truth: I wasn't hidden. I was quietly leading. It took me decades to realize that. I thought my role was to keep things running, to be the one holding it all together. And while that was true, there was more—so much more—that I wasn't acknowledging. Life has a way of shaking you awake. Sometimes gently, sometimes with a jolt you didn't see coming.

Creating a New Vision

For me, one of those jolts came when my twenty-four-year marriage ended. I still remember that weekend. I had gone away with the intention of finding ways to strengthen my marriage. I came home ready to share my ideas, but when I walked through the door, the look on his face told me everything before he said a word. I asked if he was having an affair. "No," he said, "but I'd like to." That was the moment. I told him to pack his bags. I wasn't going to keep him hostage. A month later, he moved out. After twenty-five years together, four children, and a lifetime of memories, I was stunned. And sad. Not because our relationship had been great because it hadn't been for a while, but because the future I'd pictured was gone. My vision of old age, surrounded by our children, grandchildren, maybe even great-grandchildren, all together as one happy family—that vision evaporated in a single conversation.

Once I **named** what I was truly upset about—it wasn't losing him; it was losing the family vision—I could start **reframing** it. I still had my children. We could still be a family, even if it looked different. I made deliberate choices: I wouldn't bad-mouth him to the kids. I'd keep him in the loop, even after he moved to Vegas. I'd still be an asset to our family business. I'd invite him to family events. I'd make it okay for everyone, even when it wasn't easy. And I **claimed** that vision. Fifteen years later, we celebrate holidays, birthdays, and special events together. Today, we have six grandchildren, with two more on the way and we gather often. We love each other in a way we couldn't when we were married. We are, without a doubt, better apart.

Life is never free from challenges. But I've found that when *I Name It, Frame It, Claim It*, I can navigate anything. I noticed a pattern in how I would pull myself out of a heavy state. It was a three-step dance that I performed unconsciously at first. When things felt wrong, I'd internally acknowledge what was happening. Then, I'd mentally reframe it, so it didn't overwhelm me. Finally, I'd make a conscious choice about what to do next. After years of doing this without a name, I decided to give it one. I made it an intentional practice. I started to *name it*, then I *framed it*, so that I *claimed it*. This three-step process became my lifeline, the foundation of my resilience. But I've found that when I Name It, Frame It, Claim It, I can navigate anything.

Name it: I stopped pretending things were fine when they weren't. I called it out. I got real about how I was feeling and what was happening. Even the stuff I wanted to avoid, especially that. There's power in naming something clearly and honestly. It's how you take the first step forward, refusing to let the chaos take root in the shadows. By naming the fear, the sadness, or the struggle, I stripped it of its power to control me.

Frame it: Once I could name it, I looked at how I was holding it. Was I giving this thing all my power? Was I letting it spin endlessly in my mind, taking up way more space than it deserved? Was I seeing it through old pain? Framing didn't make the hard stuff go away—but it let me hold it in a way that didn't drown me. It was a practice in perspective, a conscious choice to shift my focus from being consumed by a problem to simply observing it. It softened the grip, allowing me to see the bigger picture and find a point of stability within myself.

Claim it: This is where the shift really happens. This is where I choose what I'm going to do next. Sometimes that means action. Sometimes that means stillness. Sometimes it's just reminding myself, "This is mine, but it doesn't get to own me." Claiming it is how I keep moving, even when things are shaky. It's the ultimate act of resilience, taking ownership of my experience and my response to it. It's the final step in moving from a passive observer of my life to an active participant, ready to face whatever comes next.

In recent years, I've layered another tool into my approach: BEST. This four-step process that I lean into, BEST, is for those moments when my emotions feel too big and the spiral threatens to take over. When I'm in the middle of anxiety, uncertainty, or an emotional spiral, I use BEST. Below are the four steps you can follow too.

1. The first step is to check in with my *body/breath*. Anxiety isn't just a thought; it's a physical sensation. My throat tightens. My chest feels heavy. My breath becomes shallow and quick. Before I can address the thought, I must address the physical reality. I pause and force myself to take a slow, deep breath. Sometimes I close my eyes. I focus on the feeling of my lungs expanding, the air filling my belly. This simple act of conscious breathing acts as an anchor, pulling me back from the swirling thoughts in my head to the solid ground of my own body. It's a physiological reset button, a way to tell my nervous system, "We're okay. We're safe." I don't try to make the physical sensations go away; I simply notice them, acknowledging their presence without letting them overwhelm me.

2. Next, I move on to my *emotions*. This is where I give myself permission to be honest about what I'm truly feeling. Sad. Anxious. Frustrated. Scared. Instead of bottling these feelings up or pretending they don't exist, I name them. I might say it out loud or just to myself. "I feel anxious." "I'm scared." There is a remarkable power in naming an emotion. It's like turning on a light in a dark room: The boogeyman doesn't disappear, but you can see it for what it is, and it loses its power to control you from the shadows. The fear might still be there, but now it's anxiety, a

known quantity, not a vague, overwhelming dread. It's a crucial step in moving from being a passive victim of my feelings to an active observer of them.

3. Then comes the *self-talk*. Our minds are excellent storytellers, especially when we're feeling down. This is the stage where I challenge the narrative. I ask myself, "Is this thought true? Is it helpful? Is there another way to see this?" Often, my anxiety is fueled by worst-case scenarios and catastrophic thinking. This is where I consciously introduce a different perspective. For example, the thought might be, "This situation is going to ruin everything." My self-talk challenge is, "Is that really true? Have I faced similar situations before and gotten through them? What's a more realistic outcome?" This isn't about denying my feelings; it's about not letting a single, negative thought hijack my entire reality. It's a deliberate effort to reengage the part of my brain that knows how to problem solve rather than just panic.

4. Finally, I act. This is the crucial step that breaks the freeze mode. When we're caught in a spiral, we often feel paralyzed. The action doesn't have to be big. It can be as small as getting up and getting a glass of water or putting on a favorite song. It might be sending a text, making a list, or simply stepping outside for five minutes. The goal is to break the inertia and create forward momentum. The action itself might not solve the big problem, but it serves a vital purpose: It reminds me that I can make choices and influence my reality. It's a tangible way of claiming my power back and signaling to myself that I'm moving, even when things are shaky. It's a simple, but profound, way to get myself out of my head and back into the world.

My journey to becoming a leader and a guide for others started with the smallest of steps: a one-minute video on my social media channels. I didn't begin these daily videos on my social channels with a grand plan for a social media brand. They were just reminders to me, a little check-in with the truth. I'd add a quote, sometimes my own words, sometimes someone else's, because I wanted to hold up a moment and truly look at it. To me, those posts aren't just content. They are practice. Every single one is a moment of me *naming, framing, and claiming* something real. Sometimes raw, sometimes ordinary, but always honest. It wasn't long before people started reaching out, telling me these videos felt like a lifeline. The truth is, they were mine first.

Helping Others

This realization was a pivotal moment. I saw that my personal practice of self-awareness and resilience wasn't just for me; it had a power that could resonate with others. It was the same quiet, steady presence I had always offered, but now it was intentional, amplified, and accessible to anyone who needed it. My compass in life is a simple phrase: *The Grass Grows Where I Am*. This isn't just a saying; it's a truth I've lived by. No matter the circumstances, I've learned to bring growth, connection, and joy with me. It's not because my life has been easy, but because I've learned that joy isn't a condition of circumstance, it's a condition of choice. I call this personal awakening my enlightenment. It didn't happen on a mountaintop; it happened in the messy, middle-of-everything moments when I was holding three things in one hand, my heart in the other, and still figuring out how to keep going.

When I started to think about what I could offer others, I knew I had to look back at what shaped me. A huge part of my life, and my family's life, was a woman named Gania. She was the Polish woman who helped raise us, and while things weren't always easy in our house, she held us together. She brought a unique blend of warmth, humor, and strength. When I think of her, I think of joy. She taught me something without ever trying to: Life can be hard and beautiful at the same time. You can laugh in the middle of chaos. Gania was a living example of resilience, and her quiet strength became a part of my own. Looking back, I see how her influence and my own innate ability to be a steady presence have prepared me to help others. The skills I've cultivated—that profound ability to name a difficult truth, reframe a challenging situation, and claim a path forward—are the very tools I can now use to consult others. By sharing my journey and this simple, powerful process, I can help people navigate their own messes and find their own joy. I'm no longer just hiding in the background; I'm actively using my unique skills and experiences to guide others toward their own moments of clarity and empowerment. *As I always say: Happiness isn't something you wait for; it's something you create, even in the middle of the mess.*

This is the point in the concept of the grass growing where I truly come to life—especially when I'm at my **BEST**. When I'm grounded in my own resilience and wisdom, I can't help but create a space for others to do the same. This isn't about being perfect; it's about being present. It's about showing up for the hard moments with the same intention as the good ones. The wisdom I've cultivated isn't about avoiding pain but about learning to stand steady in its midst. It's about seeing a messy situation, not as a problem to be fixed, but as a garden to be tended. This is where my tools—**Name It, Frame It, Claim It**—become a living, breathing practice. In my experience, true resilience isn't about bouncing back from setbacks.

It's about being able to stand in the middle of the mess without losing your ground. It's a continuous choice to stay present, to not let the chaos around you define the peace within you.

I've found that my ability to bring joy and growth to any situation is directly tied to my capacity to use my framework to stay present. When I can **Name** what's truly happening, a difficult emotion or a frustrating circumstance, I refuse to let it fester in the shadows. This act of honesty immediately shifts my energy. Instead of being a victim of the moment, I become an observer of it. From there, I can **Frame** it. This isn't about putting a positive spin on something painful; it's about finding a perspective that serves my long-term well-being. It's asking myself, "How can I hold this moment in a way that doesn't drown me?" By framing the situation, I give myself power. I can see the potential lessons, the subtle shifts, and the opportunities for growth that are hidden within the discomfort. I transform a moment of potential crisis into a moment of intentional learning. And finally, I **Claim** it. This is the most empowering part of the process. Claiming it is about making a conscious choice about what to do next. Sometimes this means taking difficult action, and other times it means choosing stillness and patience. It's the ultimate act of resilience, taking ownership of my experience and my response to it. When I claim my role in the present moment, I'm planting a seed. I'm making a statement that I am not powerless. I'm affirming that I will not just survive at this moment, but I will grow from it. That's how the grass grows. It's a testament to the idea that joy and wisdom aren't just things you find; they are things you actively cultivate, one choice at a time, at every moment of your life.

Reflections for You

- When in your own life have you mistaken invisibility for safety?

- What truth about yourself have you been avoiding naming—and what might shift if you did?

- How do you usually frame challenges: as obstacles or as opportunities to grow?

- What would it look like for you to claim your voice, even in situations where you've stayed quiet before?

- How can you bring joy and steadiness into moments that feel uncertain or messy?

- Who in your life modeled resilience or wisdom for you the way Gania did for me?

- What "grass grows where I am" moment are you currently living—where you can choose to bring growth and joy right where you stand?

Connect with Ricki:

WISDOM

What "THE GRASS GROWS WHERE I AM" Means to Me

> *Our divine nature is one of wholeness and vibrancy. Deep cellular hydration brings radiant health and vitality. Join in and let's walk nature's path together where the grass grows vibrant and lush right where we are.*

Susan Brauser

Connect with Susan:

Cellular Hydration Holds the Key to Radiant Health, Smart and Simple!

Susan Brauser

The human body is magnificently designed to heal, to be vibrantly healthy, and to thrive.

I never identified as "sick," even when my body was calling out for help over so many years. I searched, trying everything to get well again—never giving up. My journey has become a sacred commitment: to live as my authentic self, to uncover profound knowledge and wisdom not only for my own healing but to light the path for others. Every health obstacle I've overcome has etched this path for me, and I offer my wholehearted gratitude for the lessons learned. My deepest conviction is rooted in the undeniable truth that the body's innate ability to heal is our divine design.

We often forget how life used to be. Growing up before these current times, serious illness was a rarity. Now, look around us. Why have we normalized a state of perpetual sickness, endless reliance on medications, and a revolving door of doctor's appointments? My healing journey has revealed a profound truth: Health and vitality aren't just something you're born with or lucky enough to enjoy.

The human body is magnificently designed to heal, to be vibrantly healthy, and to thrive. The key, I've learned, is to give your body what it needs and remove what interferes with its inherent capacity for well-being.

Self-Discovery

Having embarked on my own journey of self-discovery, I've come to learn that life is a dynamic process of exploration and growth—delving into your inner landscape, unearthing your dormant potential, and evolving into your highest, most brilliant expression. Life's challenges are not merely obstacles; they are powerful catalysts and sacred opportunities for transformation. They are the mechanisms that unlock coded messages, revealing the hidden treasures buried deep within us. What is life if not a journey of discovery? I can clearly remember a period of being "asleep" before a tick-borne disease initiated a profound awakening, which continues to this day. My journey involves navigating challenges, reaching the lowest points, working through them, and ultimately emerging into the light, forever changed. It is in these moments that the seeds of resilience and wisdom are planted.

I realized my health was too precious to blindly hand off to someone else, regardless of their credentials or perceived expertise. Instead, I became a relentless advocate for researching, for questioning, for digging deeper. This disease, encompassing both my physical illness and the challenges of the medical treatment itself, prompted me to relentlessly seek answers related to health, healing, and true learning. My quest led me from a state of complex "dis-order" and deep-seated "dis-ease" to a liberating state of simplicity and self-reliance.

I cannot emphasize enough the importance of self-advocacy. Not just for yourself, but for those you hold dear. The truths unearthed may shock, surprise, delight, and ultimately transform you as they did me. My personal journey revealed that true healing is complete and profound. It transcends the endless cycle of tips, remedies, and medicines. This is a clarion call to wake up, to remember our true divine nature as beings of inherent wholeness and radiant health. It is not just possible; it is absolutely within you. I've experienced it; we all can.

I've always considered myself a slow starter, yet my spirit has always embodied the wild embrace of nature. I cherish the raw, untamed beauty of the natural world. However, for many years, I was unaware that I didn't truly know myself, that I wasn't consciously deepening my roots to find my authentic core. This slow, steady unfolding has been my sacred path, and awareness is the master key. It is the key to an awakened life, to living consciously, creatively, and with unshakeable resilience. It's a journey of growing, transforming, and ultimately finding your true, magnificent nature.

Awareness unlocks the seemingly random patterns of life, and from this profound awakening, purpose ignites. Once you step into this illuminated state, you simply keep taking steps, relentlessly seeking out and following your bliss. This isn't a whimsical notion; it's a profound directive that resonates from the very core of your heart. Place your hand on your heart and breathe slowly, deeply. It's in that sacred connection between heart and head that truly monumental things begin to unfold.

You set in motion the planting of seeds for profound good to manifest in your life. Your state of being is paramount. Positivity, kindness, and a loving presence, these are the vital nutrients that allow everything to align in miraculous ways. There will be lessons and setbacks along the way, but we simply keep going, even when we feel we could have done better. We understand that we receive something into our energy field before it even manifests in our physical body. That's why cultivating positivity, meditating, connecting with nature, and consistently inviting in the light matters so immensely. Light brings awareness, and awareness illuminates the path.

My Path to Healing

My story, like so many journeys, began with something seemingly insignificant. It was September 1989. I was on Long Island, New York, enjoying a game of golf at Sunken Meadow Golf Course, a place known for its narrow fairways that inevitably led me into the "rough" surrounded by tall, overgrown grass. I remember a full-sized photo of a tick at the entrance, a silent warning. But my only prior experience was with the sizable dog ticks from the woods in my childhood. I had no concept of the tiny, almost invisible creatures capable of carrying such potent illnesses. I was "asleep" to the profound shift that was about to utterly transform my life.

Ten days later, a high fever gripped me, followed by a bizarre, random joint pain in a single finger—so specific, so unusual. A fleeting news report on Lyme disease must have sparked something, for I found myself at the library, devouring every scrap of information about my strange new symptoms. Armed with this knowledge, I approached an internist and asked to be tested for Lyme. His dismissive response still echoes: "You probably have rheumatoid arthritis." But I knew he was wrong; it simply didn't feel right. My insistence paid off. The test came back positive for Lyme. I was fortunate to receive that early diagnosis, especially given Lyme testing's notoriously unreliable nature.

For three years, I managed the illness with yearly antibiotics, believing I was being reinfected each summer. Then, it hit me full-blown. The symptoms were intense, relentless: debilitating joint pains, absolute mental and physical exhaustion. I began continuous antibiotic treatment at Lenox Hill Hospital, in New York City. Symptoms lessened, offering a fleeting reprieve. A couple of months later, the internist declared that I was free of Lyme, claiming I now had "autoimmune Lyme." My question was simple, yet profound: "If I no longer have Lyme, why do I feel better on antibiotics?"

The answer would take years to reveal itself: Medicines suppress symptoms; they do not confer true healing. Reducing symptoms is too often tragically confused with genuine healing. This has far-reaching implications and is the most common state that people are in. As symptoms are being managed, they are headed further away from true health and healing. Unwilling to accept this simplistic narrative of a new diagnosis, not yet understanding symptom suppression versus regaining health, I sought a Lyme specialist who treated aggressively with antibiotics. I stayed with that doctor for a year, receiving high doses of oral antibiotics, injections, and IVs.

Through a Lyme support group, I learned of a father in California who had researched and built a Rife healing energy machine to treat his family's Lyme disease. The book *The Cancer Cure That Worked* by Barry Lynes was recommended to me. I devoured this remarkable account of Royal Raymond Rife's 1930s breakthroughs. I stopped the IVs, and my husband drove me to the Adirondacks to meet the beautiful fellow seeker, Dan Tracy. He had built his own Rife machine, dedicating decades to helping others. He opened his home, offering treatment and building machines for people worldwide. He built one for me. After several weeks, I felt noticeably better but needed an hour of daily treatment to maintain feeling better.

My search for a cure continued. I tried everything, but nothing truly healed. I was blessed to be part of a vibrant community; information sharing became my way out. In 1995, I found Dr. Brody, a naturopath who used a Vega machine, an old-time diagnostic tool that tested for frequency. With his remedies, I finally began to feel better, and within six months, I was well. Several years later, in 2003, I was reinfected by another tick bite. For eleven years, quarterly hair samples sent to a bioresonance practitioner guided my remedies, and I felt relatively well. But when I tried to stop all my symptoms came rushing back.

Overwhelmed by my husband's escalating health challenges brought on by an automobile accident, I desperately sought help, a broadening of focus that led to a truly meaningful turning point. In December 2012, I attended an introductory meeting for the Bruno Gröning Circle of Friends, a worldwide, volunteer-run, community dedicated to healing on the spiritual path through the teaching of Bruno Gröning. Bruno Gröning, known as the "Miracle Healer" after World War II in Germany, died in 1959, yet healings continue through the group's work and documented healing reports. The presentation and music were so profoundly moving that tears were streaming down my face. Then, the community leader shared her own Lyme healing story.

I immersed myself, attending community hours, special events, and practicing daily "Einstellen," the profound act of taking in the Heilstrom, or healing stream. From the moment I joined, I felt a deep sense of grounding and immense support, a stark contrast to the isolation I had endured. Nearly two years later, in late October 2014, I experienced a remarkable healing. I suddenly stopped taking my remedies and felt truly well, experiencing a noticeable boost in vitality. It was a liberating feeling, a taste of true independence after twenty-five years of unyielding reliance on remedies. Today, approximately 6,000 medical practitioners within this circle meticulously examine healing reports, attributing these miracles to the Heilstrom, or Divine Source energy.

> *There is no incurable!*
> —Bruno Gröning

Cellular Hydration

In May 2015, I discovered Darko Velcek's profound work on healing through cellular hydration. My experience with Darko's protocol was a revelation: the unconventional, yet undeniable truth of how the body truly heals. The day I found his work, I was bedridden with my back "out"—the third time that year. Reading Dr. Mercola's newsletter, I delved into the comments and found Darko's intriguing explanation. I contacted him, had a fascinating conversation, read his ebooks, *Owner's Manual for the Human Body* and *Self-Healers Protocol*, and immediately began his cellular hydration protocol. For two weeks, my body adjusted to the process of hydration and detoxification—two sides of the same vital coin. After this initial period, my cleansing symptoms were minimal, and my energy was markedly better. I was on the path to greater health and vitality. And that, remarkably, was the last time my back relegated me to bed.

This was my first true introduction to the concept that water is so much more than just H2O. Structured water was central to the teachings, alongside rarely known truths about food, water, medicines, and our body's intricate workings. This protocol resonated deeply, emphasizing the fundamental pillars of health: food, water, nature, and self-trust. I found it incredibly valuable, especially its focus on structuring water and adding a wet, unrefined sea salt to create "plasma." "Plasma" is the fundamental key to cellular hydration, its minerals in the perfect proportion for absorption, mirroring our own blood plasma. We are electrical beings; when a cell is fully charged, it is vitally healthy and functions optimally. When conditions are right for deep cellular hydration, our cells freely open to release toxic waste and hydrate.

The salt needed for maintaining the correct level of blood "plasma" is a wet unrefined sea salt that is electrically charged and contains ninety-plus minerals and trace elements. The only source where this salt can be found is recently evaporated seawater, naturally sun-dried, with nothing added or removed. It's very rich in magnesium salts and other essential minerals. This salt provides vital nourishment, conferring a wealth of health properties. Without it, we suffer from dehydration. Most salt, including "sea salt" mined from the earth, is not sea salt but is a rock salt, very low in magnesium and other essential minerals.

Darko meticulously explains the body's inner workings, what is needed for hydration, and why. If the salt we need is insufficient, the body will not be able to hold adequate levels of water because it cannot achieve the correct electroconductivity. Plasma is the electroconductive state of water achieved through mineralization. Low levels of plasma make the body reluctant to cleanse the blood because it cannot afford to lose plasma. The blood remains toxic and slowly over time toxins get deposited in tissues, increasing the overall toxicity of the body. The more toxic the blood, the more closed the cellular membranes become, preventing hydration on a cellular level. And when "toxic" substances circulate, cells shut down to keep them out. Many seemingly "healthy" foods and medicinal substances, I learned, are surprisingly incompatible with cellular hydration. Once I grasped the profound "why," embracing this path became seamless.

For years, I had sought answers, meticulously researching and pursuing endless healing modalities and treatments. My newfound understanding, the true key to health, healing, and optimum vitality, lies in cellular hydration. While not difficult to implement, hydrating at the cellular level is far more intricate than simply drinking water. Darko's brilliant work provides anyone interested with the essential information to begin and achieve optimal hydration. Today, as so many unwittingly move deeper into dehydration, I gratefully share the information and wisdom I've gathered on this transformative healing journey.

Structured Water

Two years after discovering Darko's Protocol, in 2017, while searching for a new water system, I was introduced to Natural Action's water structuring products. I devoured the information and was captivated. It led me to realize that water in its natural state is the elixir of life and the path to vibrant well-being. I began with Natural Action's portable revitalizer, using it for several months before investing in their other products. The experience was so compelling that I became deeply involved, and today I am a partner in the company that researches, engineers, and manufactures these remarkable tools. The products are designed to hydrate, detoxify, and profoundly revitalize the body.

My entire perspective on water shifted dramatically. I had always known water was essential, but I came to understand that it is so much more. It's not merely a collection of molecules; it is vital, life-giving, and carries profound energy. When properly structured, when truly revitalized, water undergoes a profound molecular change. This structured water isn't just hydrating; it's communicating, unifying, and harmonizing. In essence, water is life itself.

My experience with the structured water mirrored Darko's hydration protocol. It took two weeks to fully integrate the structuring of all my drinking water. I paced myself to find a comfortable balance with detoxifying symptoms, and after two weeks, my energy and clarity soared.

It's now been a few years since integrating structured water with the hydration protocol and the results have been remarkable. My health, vitality, and mental clarity are consistently excellent. Some of what I've experienced while reclaiming my health is: deep, restorative sleep—waking up refreshed and energized free of pain and discomfort; clear mental acuity; a trimmer, fitter body; and renewed emotional resilience and zest for life. This transformation stems from a fundamental understanding that the body is constantly striving to cleanse itself, however, it absolutely requires proper hydration to do so effectively. Without it, the body struggles to eliminate toxins—its ability to properly cleanse is compromised, and that's when we experience symptoms that show up as "conditions," "illnesses," and "diseases."

By providing the body with the hydration it needs, you empower its innate healing mechanisms. While this is a process—after all, discomforts didn't appear overnight—the journey is an upward spiral. There will be periods of cleansing as your body clears out toxins. You may experience some symptoms such as tiredness, but these are signs of healing, leading you toward a healthier, more vibrant you. Simply, food, water, and minerals are all I take to achieve and maintain my level of wellness. Spiritual practice and connecting with nature remain foundational for me.

Natural Action, utilizing biomimicry, uses *flow form* technology to emulate nature's own process of cleansing and structuring water. These flow forms are specially designed to create multiple dual vortexes that spin simultaneously in opposite directions as water passes through. Furthermore, the flow forms are imbued with rare earth materials, which impart a high vibrational resonance into the water. This powerful combination of vortexing and frequency infusion results in a highly qualitative state of water structuring and revitalizing.

Think of a pristine mountain stream—the water is refreshing, vibrant, alive. This is because it's constantly flowing, tumbling, and being energized. Contrast that with water sitting stagnant in pipes or bottles; it becomes "dormant," losing its inherent vitality. In the pursuit of "clean" water, many unknowingly drink energetically "dead" water, or worse, water whose molecular structure has been scrambled. Structuring water after these purifying methods restores its natural coherence. If your water is treated with electricity—ionized, reverse osmosis, or distilled water—its molecular structure is severely disrupted and needs to be brought back into coherence. These electrical processes are unnatural. Structured water, however, is abundant in nature wherever water flows freely. The more flow and vortexing, the more coherent, energized, vital, and cleansed the water becomes.

When your cells are properly hydrated, they are fully charged, and your body's innate healing mechanism is optimized.

Cultivating Resilient Health

I learned that all the water within our cells is naturally structured. If you're not drinking structured water, especially when unwell, your body expends precious energy to revitalize "lifeless" water on its own. This constant internal effort diverts vital resources away from healing and thriving. This is the very core of my message, which I now widely share: Cultivating resilient health ultimately comes down to cellular hydration. When your cells are properly hydrated, they are fully charged, and your body's innate healing mechanisms are optimized. It's like giving your cells the ultimate super fuel, empowering them to perform at their peak.

My journey is a perpetual process of learning and deepening my understanding of what it truly means to be well. For decades, I lived trapped in a cycle of seeking external solutions to manage my health. I understand the frustration, the despair, and the sheer mental and emotional exhaustion that comes with feeling unwell yet tirelessly seeking answers. Structured water can step in as a powerful ally for your own sacred journey. Imagine your cells, the very building blocks of your body, no longer struggling to hydrate themselves. Imagine them effortlessly absorbing the life-giving energy of water, just as nature divinely intended.

By simply choosing to empower yourself with cellular hydration, you're providing your system with the fundamental support it needs to heal, to regenerate, and to thrive. You are enabling deep, cellular wellness that conventional approaches tragically overlook. It's an act of profound self-advocacy, a return to your true, divine blueprint of health.

I invite you to fearlessly explore this vital truth. You don't have to navigate the complexities of chronic illness alone, nor do you have to settle for merely "getting by." Embrace the simplicity and profound power of cellular hydration, and witness firsthand how this foundational change can ripple through every aspect of your well-being, empowering you to embark on your own magnificent journey back to vibrant health and cultivating unshakeable resiliency.

There are countless beautiful testimonials for both Darko's work and Natural Action's structured water devices. I am eternally thankful to have found my way to true health, vitality, and vibrancy through this transformative healing journey. Are you ready to experience these remarkable changes for yourself? I wholeheartedly invite you to embark on a journey of *your* own, so that the grass can truly grow, vibrant and lush, right where you stand.

Your Next Step

My healing journey has brought me full circle from being "sick" to a place of vibrant health and wholeness. It is my desire to share everything I've learned along the way with fellow seekers of lasting health who are ready to empower themselves with this knowledge. May life bring you radiant health, deepening experiences, and the quest for truth.

If you would like to learn more on how to bring cellular hydration into your life, receive further guidance, or connect with fellow seekers, join us on Skool in the Self Healers Protocol SHP community.

My journey has become a sacred commitment: to live as my authentic self, to uncover profound knowledge and wisdom not only for my own healing but to light the path for others.

Reflections for You

- Has your understanding of hydration and its impact on overall health changed after reading about the role of cellular hydration in healing?

- What do you think about the possibility of healing a multitude of conditions and feeling truly well? Do you believe it is possible? What would that look like for you?

- In what ways can embracing self-advocacy and nurturing your body's innate healing mechanisms empower you on your own journey toward resilient health?

- What would it mean to hold the wisdom and knowledge of self-trust and deep healing?

- What does "our divine nature is one of wholeness and vibrancy" mean to you?

Connect with Susan:

What "THE GRASS GROWS WHERE I AM" Means to Me

> *Doing what I do with my whole heart— and blooming wherever I'm planted.*

Dr. Kathy Brooks Holloway

Connect with Dr. Kathy:

The Earth's Whisper: A Journey of Wisdom and Resilience

Dr. Kathy Brooks Holloway

Treat the earth well—We do not inherit the earth from our ancestors; we borrow it from our children.

—Native American proverb

From the earliest days of my childhood, long before I truly understood its profound implications, I was captivated by the mesmerizing world depicted in *National Geographic* documentaries. Weekends were often spent immersed in incredible indigenous ecosystems and the majestic narratives of ancient civilizations. What truly resonated, burrowing deep into my young spirit, was the subtle yet powerful story of how these people lived in such profound harmony with nature. They didn't merely exist within their environments; they understood its intricate rhythms, relying on the land, not just for their needs, but as a living, breathing entity from which all wisdom flowed.

The indigenous peoples, with their deep reverence and innate understanding, passed down nature's "secrets" through countless generations. These "secrets" were wisdoms that, I believe, are innate in all of us, lying dormant, waiting to be rediscovered. I felt the Earth itself was speaking, whispering the wisdom of ages, echoing through time if we would only slow down and truly listen.

I recall the simple, yet profound, act of being barefoot on the ground. There was an immediate, almost magical, sensation of negative thoughts discharging, a tangible connection back to the very essence of the earth. It was as if I were a sponge, soaking up the boundless love of the earth around me, accepting these truths as my own. This absorption was filtered, amplified, and made deeply personal through the eyes of my Native American grandmother. Her quiet wisdom, her intuitive connection to the land shaped me into becoming a naturalist.

Stewards of the Earth

That early fascination with the innate rhythm of nature wasn't just a fleeting interest; it planted a tiny seed within me that has since grown, steadily and mightily, into a resilient oak. My inherent belief, nurtured by my grandmother's teachings and my own observations, crystallized: We are, unequivocally, stewards of the earth. This realization was a profound self-discovery that gently but firmly led me back to the practice of grounding, to a conscious reconnection with the earth beneath my feet. Today, I live with immense gratitude and a deep, abiding love for the earth, finding an abundance of joy in the natural rhythms that permeate every aspect of life. Through practicing love and forgiveness as a constant reset, I allow myself to release what no longer serves me, approaching each day unburdened, with a fresh perspective for my well-being and for living life to its fullest potential. This isn't just a philosophy; it's the rhythm of my being.

As I transitioned into young adulthood, embarking on my journey in the Navy, my understanding of health and the environment took on a much more urgent and personal dimension. It was during this period that doctors acknowledged significant deficiencies and toxic loads in my body, directly linked to where I had been raised and living in rural Georgia, specifically the area farms impacted by continuous cotton farming practices. Furthermore, they identified toxins from the relentless chemical exchanges associated with manufacturing and the widespread use of synthetic fertilizers in commercial farming.

This stark, personal revelation was a wake-up call, profoundly reshaping my appreciation for the vital role of dense nutrition. I came to see that these fundamental nutrients weren't just about physical health, fueling our bodies, and preventing disease but were the foundational building blocks for emotional stability and the very development of healthy lifestyle practices. It became strikingly clear that without proper cellular nourishment, our bodies are inherently compromised. Our emotional and physical resilience fades, making us exponentially more susceptible to stress, imbalance, and eventually, a cascade of diseases.

I see it all around us: Our modern diet has become tragically nutrient poor. We consume an abundance of calories, often from highly processed foods laden with sugars and unhealthy fats, yet, ironically, our cells are literally starving for the vital vitamins and minerals they desperately need to thrive. This nutritional deficit isn't merely about feeling tired or a bit sluggish; it is, in my firm belief, the root cause of so many of the chronic health challenges we face today. From pervasive inflammation and debilitating digestive issues to complex autoimmune disorders, the threads connect back to this fundamental lack.

My conviction is strong: The rising rates of cancers, a shadow that looms over so many lives, have a profound connection to this lack of nutrition and the escalating toxic loads we are exposed to. These come not only from modern farming practices but also from added preservatives, synthetic fertilizers, and the ubiquitous presence of plastics in our everyday environments. The human body, a complex and self-repairing marvel, demands a precise array of nutrients for optimal performance. *Dense nutrition is the foundational cornerstone upon which every cellular function depends, the very bricks and mortar of health.* This profound understanding sparked an intense fascination, driving me to explore the intricate world of herbal medicine. Discovering the remarkable ability of specific herbs to bolster organ function and efficiently neutralize harmful substances for removal has been transformative. This knowledge has completely reshaped my perspective on conventional healthcare, unveiling a pathway to genuine wellness and robustness, enduring health.

With this newfound clarity and a deep personal understanding, my intention is now crystal clear and unwavering: to actively explore and implement solutions that nurture both ourselves and the earth and that work intimately with nature. My inspiration continues to be those captivating *National Geographic* specials, where ancient civilizations didn't just survive but thrived, creating entire societies right outside their doors, in perfect symbiotic relationship with their environment.

This chapter of my life, therefore, is not merely an intellectual pursuit; it is a profound exploration of moving forward with both wisdom and resilience. It demands a deep introspection, a careful listening to the myriad influences that have shaped us and consciously discerning and choosing the principles that will authentically guide us. More than that, it's about actively participating in shaping a future—a future where both individual well-being and the holistic health of our communities are not just considerations but paramount objectives. Ultimately, it's about recognizing that within each of us lies an innate capacity for change, a powerful force that, when harnessed, can embrace the power of intention to shape the world around us. And that transformation, that profound shift, must begin from within us.

Permaculture

This brings me to another immensely powerful concept that has become a guiding star in my journey: permaculture. At its heart, permaculture is the art and science of designing with nature in mind. It's a complete departure from the extractive, linear systems that have dominated modern agriculture and development. The absolute starting point for any successful permaculture design is deep observation. This isn't a casual glance; it's a patient, immersive study of the land. It involves truly understanding the natural flow of water across the landscape, discerning the intricate patterns of sunlight throughout the day and across the changing seasons, feeling the prevailing winds, and meticulously noting the existing features of the landscape, including native plants and indigenous wildlife. This careful, almost meditative observation is what truly informs the design, ensuring that it works seamlessly with nature's inherent patterns, rather than imposing artificial structures upon them.

One of the foundational techniques we utilize in permaculture, designed directly from this deep observation, involves "swales." These are carefully dug trenches on contour lines, designed not to drain water away but to capture and gently slow down rainwater. The Native Indians constructed swales on the mountaintop property where I live. The original design allows the precious water to percolate slowly and deeply into the soil, recharging vital groundwater reserves, rather than run off and cause erosion and the tragic depletion of nutrients. "Berms" are the complementary earth mounds created from the very soil dug from these swales. These berms serve as initial steps to recharge the soils, prevent further erosion, and critically create unique microclimates—small, sheltered areas that are ideal planting material for specific trees, such as fruit trees.

My studies and travels have shown me incredible examples of permaculture in action. In Africa, for instance, the keyhole garden stands out as an exceptionally efficient design. It's a planned circular garden bed with a central compost pile that constantly feeds nutrients outward to the surrounding plants. This simple yet ingenious design maximizes space and efficiency, creating a highly productive system. Another cornerstone of permaculture is its reliance on "companion planting."

The wisdom of communities like the Amish, who use natural pest repellents that are tried and true, exemplifies this principle perfectly. It involves strategically positioning different species together, knowing they will benefit one another. For example, planting marigolds near tomato plants can effectively deter common pests, while basil is known to sweeten the flavor of nearby tomatoes. Legumes, through a natural process, can fix nitrogen in the soil, providing essential nutrients that benefit nearby plants. Some plants offer protective canopy, shading the soil and retaining precious moisture, while others act as natural pesticides or herbicides, suppressing unwanted growth without harmful chemicals.

Permaculture teaches us that pests can be deterred naturally, and shading the soil is a simple, effective way to retain moisture. It also, unequivocally, entails using natural pest control methods, like stewed tobacco or diatomaceous earth, instead of resorting to harmful synthetic chemicals. And for fertilizers, we go back to basics, embracing the wisdom of nutrient cycling: rich worm castings from compost piles will all be diligently added back to the soil. This replenishes the earth, improving its structure and fertility, and ensuring the growth of truly nutrient-dense foods, rich in the full spectrum of minerals our bodies so desperately need. Vitally, animals are also an integral part of a healthy permaculture system, contributing to soil health, pest control, and nutrient cycling in a balanced way.

Hemp

As I delve deeper into truly sustainable solutions, one plant stands out with remarkable potential: hemp. While cotton has enjoyed immense popularity and widespread use for centuries, its production comes with significant, undeniable disadvantages. It is, alarmingly, an incredibly thirsty crop, demanding vast amounts of water and often grown in arid regions where water resources are already scarce, contributing significantly to the tragic phenomenon of desertification. Beyond its voracious water appetite, cotton production is notoriously pesticide intensive. These harmful chemicals seep into groundwater, devastate biodiversity, and pose severe health risks not only to the farm workers who toil in the fields but also to nearby, downstream communities whose water sources become contaminated.

A healthier, profoundly more sustainable, and environmentally friendly option is hemp. This is a plant with a staggering 100 percent usefulness, literally from its seeds to its stalks. It's significantly more sustainable and environmentally friendly than cotton in every measurable aspect. Consider hemp fodder, for example. It's a complete food for animals, offering a naturally made, balanced diet without the myriad of toxins often found in processed animal feed.

Our animals, sadly, are currently eating foods laden with artificial colors and by-products, which contributes to a toxic load that then inevitably affects us when we consume their meat or dairy products. By feeding our animals hemp, it is 100 percent natural, ensuring no toxic load will be passed on to them and, consequently, to us.

Hemp requires far less water to grow and matures much faster, yielding significantly more fiber per acre than cotton. Furthermore, hemp naturally possesses remarkable antibacterial properties, resisting mold, mildew, and fungi without any chemical intervention. It is inherently resistant to most insects and grows so densely that it naturally outcompetes weeds, reducing the need for herbicides. Because hemp has incredible versatility and strength, it is now being rapidly embraced and utilized in the transportation community, including automotive and aviation industries, and is becoming widely recognized as a revolutionary material in the building community. Imagine the future: building homes with hempcrete, a truly sustainable building material that is breathable, mold-resistant, fire-resistant, and provides excellent insulation—a natural, healthy alternative to conventional building materials laden with chemicals.

Eco-Building & The Farm Vision: Designing Resilience

A sustainable future necessitates a return to ancient, eco-friendly building methods like cob or adobe, using readily available, non-toxic earth materials. This millennia-old technique offers durability, affordability, and minimal environmental impact, harmonizing natural building with modern design and technology. As a new start-up farm, retreat, and learning center, we will be exploring innovative approaches, including hemp-based bricks, handmade or machine-produced, 3-D printing, and straw bale insulation, maximizing energy efficiency and resource utilization. Experimentation is key; everything is a learning opportunity.

The early whisper from those *National Geographic* documentaries has truly grown into a resounding call back to nature, bringing my journey full circle. My most immediate and tangible dream is to transform the eight acres where I live on a mountaintop, the highest elevation in this area in Georgia, into an innovative, sustainable farm and learning center. Here, we will actively explore and implement techniques that work in harmony with nature, such as cultivating and utilizing hemp, and building structures strategically below the frostline. This method leverages the Earth's constant temperature, which would naturally reduce the need for excessive heating and cooling, offering inherent energy efficiency.

My son, Jack, and I had a deeply inspiring visit to Taos, New Mexico, where we experienced the renowned Earthship community. We saw firsthand a lot of the same practices and concepts put into action: These off-grid homes utilize principles like those of the Amish, including incredible thermal mass to preserve heat and maintain comfortable indoor temperatures year-round. The overarching goal is to create a home environment that is inherently protected from extreme weather events, is fireproof, and provides profound resilience and self-sufficiency for its inhabitants.

A cornerstone of true sustainability lies in our relationship with water. In my vision, harvesting and water catchment systems will be paramount, allowing us to reuse all available water, including black and gray water, for a truly sustainable solution. This approach not only makes a significantly smaller environmental footprint but also directly limits our exposure to extreme weather fluctuations and the potential for insufficient water supplies. My aspiration is to construct these earth-based residences, not merely as shelters, but as dynamic learning environments fostering education in harmonious partnership with the natural world.

Supplementing the primary living areas, I envisage rustic cottages providing tranquil havens for participants in retreats designed for agriculturalists, families, and nature enthusiasts, ensuring the project's enduring vitality. *My goal is to secure funding for the foundational seed money we need to make these beautiful cabins that will sustain the project.* Donations will get us off the ground, and income from renting the cabins to participants will ensure long-term sustainability. These charming cabins will fully immerse guests in the surrounding ecosystem, exposing them to vibrant flora, bountiful orchards, and verdant thickets that will culminate in the simple delight of partaking in nature's unadulterated abundance.

I have already begun this work, having dug an eight-foot-deep trench on my property. This trench harnesses the earth's constant temperature to heat a geothermal nursery, where we will grow food using graywater from the kitchen sink, showers, tubs, and laundry. Barrels collecting rainwater in the nursery will also play a crucial role in helping to control the temperature and humidity. In the summer, when the hot air rises, a strategically placed south facing window can be opened to create a natural suction, drawing cooler air from where the geothermal pipe comes into the nursery. But in the winter, the sun will warm the water and stone elements within the nursery, and at night, these elements will slowly release that stored heat, allowing for a steady, constant temperature ideal for year-long growth.

On my land, all these practices will be an immersive, hands-on experience for anyone visiting. During your stay, while we create, design, and build unique earthen homes, your lodging will be a geodome, yurt, tree house, or wooden cabin, all offering a harmonious blend of nature with modern comfort. By offering diverse living environments, I hope to spark within everyone who visits a profound love of nature and a renewed appreciation for sustainable living. Envision a tranquil, deeply immersive natural setting where families, farmers, and the entire community undergo a profound shift, embracing a simpler, more sustainable existence. This vision is further augmented by my fervent pursuit of cutting-edge technologies, such as atmospheric water generators capable of harvesting substantial quantities of water daily, thereby bolstering our self-reliance and optimizing resource utilization.

Cultivating Vibrant, Resilient Communities

My vision extends beyond the boundaries of my own land; it encompasses the cultivation of vibrant, resilient communities. We can establish easily accessible community compost hubs where food scraps, fallen leaves, tree trimmings, and other organic matter are collected and transformed back into nutrient-rich, living soil. These centers would be vibrant places for sharing knowledge, exploring new ideas, researching ancient techniques, offering hands-on opportunities for learning, and fostering genuine collaboration for community building. Critically, these hubs would also be places for learning even from failures because that humble acceptance and adaptation are vital to success in sustainable gardening and, indeed, in community building itself.

With hands-on experiences, this retreat will be empowering for families, for individuals attending retreats, or simply for those who just want to be in nature, providing that vital connection that has been stripped away from our manicured landscapes and industrialized lives. Through workshops and events on this farm, your family will discover new ideas, learning ecological water reuse and practical, nature-based buildings and homesteading. At the same time, we'll be limiting the exposure to the chemicals and toxins normally used for building and planting while promoting the profound joy and health benefits of harvesting directly from the ground. By exploring and drawing inspiration from communities like the Amish and indigenous peoples, by working intimately with nature through permaculture farms, by consciously limiting our exposures to toxins, and by considering hemp not only in our building but also as a toxic-free food, we can genuinely learn ways to drastically limit the chemicals we introduce into our bodies and our homes.

On my land in Georgia, I am committed to collaborating with builders and developers, with philanthropic organizations, and with the wider community to incorporate sustainable and regenerative design principles into all new constructions and renovations. Furthermore, we can actively encourage the creation of earth homes and root cellars for natural food storage and climate control, dramatically reducing our reliance on energy intensive refrigeration and heating systems. Imagine entire communities designed with permaculture principles at their very core, where every single home contributes positively to a healthier ecosystem, minimizes its environmental footprint, and fosters a deeper, more profound connection to the earth.

This is the future I envision: a future where our food is protected and pure, our communities are resilient and supportive, and our planet can sustain us vibrantly for generations to come. Creating a world where "the grass grows where I am" is more than just a hopeful mantra to me; it is a living testament to the thriving life and positive impact that only true collaboration can bring. It's time to move beyond the limiting confines of competition and wholeheartedly embrace collaboration for the sake of our collective well-being and, indeed, for the very future. My vision extends far beyond individual wellness; it encompasses the holistic health of our communities near and far.

That early whisper from *National Geographic*, carrying the ancient wisdom of nature and civilization's past, has grown into a resounding call to action. We possess the knowledge, we have the tools, and collectively, we hold the immense capacity to build a future where vibrant health is the norm, not the exception, where flourishing is the standard.

Cultivate the Future: Join Us in Building This Essential Learning Haven

This future, I firmly believe, begins with you. I urge you to join me in transforming this sustainable farm into a vibrant reality. Just as I learned invaluable lessons from my grandmother, you too can have a similar, profound experience. Imagine a garden where children and adults alike can get their hands into the soil, fostering a deep connection to the earth. This hands-on learning will empower generations by cultivating a true understanding of food and holistic well-being and fostering practical self-reliance. This farm will be a center point for teaching life-sustaining skills, empowering individuals, and cultivating an unwavering connection to nature that conventional practices have systematically stripped away.

Let's build a future with a profound and lasting impact on how we live. We're creating an essential learning haven on this farm, and we need your help. Your contributions will directly fund the vital resources required: lodging, building materials, tools, expert-led workshops, and crucial community engagement programs. With every dollar, you're not just funding a project; you're cultivating healthier individuals, fostering thriving communities, and contributing to a truly sustainable future. Whether it's through financial contributions, volunteering your skills, sharing your knowledge, or simply spreading the word, your involvement will be a powerful force for change. Join us in cultivating a vibrant, flourishing environment where our collective efforts can truly blossom. This farm—Bella Healing Gardens—will stand as a living testament to our shared commitment to collaborative community building, resilience, and a genuinely regenerative future.

Through Bella Healing Gardens, we're inspired to nurture both nature and community with purpose and connection. When we give back with love—through our time, creativity, and care—life around us thrives, becoming brighter, stronger, and more beautiful wherever we are planted.

Reflections for You

- How can you connect with the earth in your community daily?

- How would teaching children to grow their own food contribute to the planet?

- What does it feel like to eat nutrient-dense food you have grown in your own backyard?

- Do you think composting is a worthwhile endeavor to add value to the soil?

- How will doing your part now to help in our soil's recovery process help future generations to flourish?

Connect with Dr. Kathy:

What "THE GRASS GROWS WHERE I AM" Means to Me

> When we come into this world we are like a seed of grass with all we need to grow into our full potential. With some self care and nurturing, we will reach our full growth. A blade of grass does not worry about the wind or rain, it only uses them to grow and get stronger. So why can't we?

Dr. Steven Crane

Connect with Dr. Steven:

Peace or Frustration: The Choice Is Yours

Dr. Steven Crane, DMD

*Rule number one is, don't sweat the small stuff.
Rule number two is, it's all small stuff.*

—Dr. Robert S. Eliot

In this fast-paced, complicated world, it's way too easy to get swept away in the minutia of life and forget the bigger picture. I have found that if you change your focus, you can and will change your life. We've given up so much control in our lives, forgetting that we control our focus and therefore our peace, joy, and experience of love. Like anything else, changing your focus takes dedication and practice. It's a muscle that needs consistent exercise, a path you can choose to walk every single day. Have you ever noticed how some people seem to glide through life with an unshakeable calm while others are perpetually caught in a storm of their own making? The difference often lies in their conscious choice between peace and frustration.

Frustration is a pervasive, insidious force. It begins subtly, perhaps with a minor inconvenience such as a slow driver, a delayed flight, a misspoken word. But if we allow it, it rapidly escalates.

Your thoughts become agitated, your breathing shallows, and your muscles tense. You replay the irritating event again, feeding the negativity until it becomes a roaring fire within you. This internal inferno doesn't just affect your mood; it spills over into every interaction. You might snap at loved ones, perform poorly at work, or even neglect your own well-being. Frustration narrows your vision, trapping you in a cycle of blame and reactivity. It tells you the world is happening *to* you, that you are a victim of circumstance, powerless to alter your emotional state. It's a heavy, draining cloud that obscures joy and suffocates connection.

Choosing Peace

Conversely, choosing peace is an act of profound self-empowerment. It's not about ignoring life's challenges or pretending everything is perfect. Peace is the calm eye of the storm, the ability to remain centered amid chaos. When you choose peace, you acknowledge difficulties but refuse to let them dictate your inner state. This involves a conscious shift in perspective. Instead of dwelling on what's wrong, you can seek understanding, practice acceptance, and look for solutions. Peace widens your lens, allowing you to see the interconnectedness of things and to respond thoughtfully rather than react impulsively. It fosters empathy, compassion, and resilience. Imagine encountering that slow driver, but instead of fuming, you use the moment to take a few deep breaths, slow down, and get centered.

How can you look at this in a way that evokes peace? Maybe the frustrating person allowed you to avoid the upcoming accident or experience something magical that you otherwise would not have. The possibilities are endless. It recognizes that while external events may be beyond your control, your internal response is always your sovereign territory. The sustained cultivation of peace leads to an abundance of joy and a deeper, richer experience of love. It allows you to approach every moment, every relationship, every challenge, from a place of strength and clarity rather than from a place of tension and irritation. This choice, fundamentally, shapes the quality of your entire existence.

My early understanding of peace, and its stark contrast to frustration, began right in my childhood home. I witnessed firsthand how my mom would often stress and get anxious about her friendships and how she perceived her friends were relating to her. It was a cycle that often led to heartbreak. She would overthink interactions, misinterpret silences, and frequently end up sabotaging relationships. I saw her drop friends abruptly, become deeply suspicious of others' intentions, and ultimately spiral into sadness, anger, or profound frustration. To witness my mom in such constant emotional turmoil was incredibly difficult. It cast a long shadow, and even at a young age, it solidified a deep-seated resolve within me: I never wanted to inhabit that emotional space. That powerful observation became the genesis of my personal journey, a conscious decision to become someone who does not fall prey to emotional chaos or negativity.

Fortunately, when I was young, I wasn't just observing; I was also escaping into the rich worlds of fantasy and science fiction books. These stories weren't just entertainment; they were blueprints for resilience and purpose. I found myself profoundly relating to characters who were consistently kind, deeply caring, and relentlessly dedicated to making a significant difference in their fictional worlds. These were heroes who faced insurmountable odds, yet their core remained unshaken. I started to understand a critical truth: To accomplish what they were after, whether it was saving a kingdom, discovering a new galaxy, or simply protecting their loved ones, they needed an extreme focus on the truly important aspects of their goals and dreams. There were no distractions, no excuses for them. They simply never let anger, frustration, or pettiness get in the way of their overarching mission. This wasn't just about strength; it was about unwavering mental discipline.

Building Emotional Intelligence

Inspired by these fictional titans, I set out to embody their essence in my own life. It became an active pursuit. I delved into meditation cassette tapes and CDs, immersing myself in guided practices that taught me to quiet the incessant chatter of my mind. I devoured self-help books, absorbing wisdom from authors who articulated the principles of emotional mastery and positive psychology. I also became a keen observer of real-life examples, people like Leo Buscaglia, whose infectious love for humanity radiated from every word, and Marianne Williamson, whose profound spiritual insights offered a path to inner peace.

Looking back, I didn't explicitly call it "building emotional intelligence" then, but that's precisely what I was doing. I was diligently feeding my mind with examples of how I wanted to be, consciously choosing my mental diet to cultivate peace, happiness, and love. As I continued this path, I started noticing patterns in how people, including my mom, would express themselves in ways that often felt hurtful or unproductive. I vividly remember countless instances when my mom would berate my dad for one thing or another, and I could physically see the energy drain from him, his demeanor shifting into one of quiet resignation. My heart ached for him in those moments. That observation burned another truth into my consciousness: I never wanted to make anyone feel like that.

What was equally clear, though, was that beneath her frustration, she loved him very much and was immensely proud of him for so many things. It was a disconnect. I came to the profound understanding that she was simply expressing herself in a way that was not aligned with what she genuinely wanted to accomplish. She just wanted him to do something different, perhaps to be heard or understood, but she didn't have to put him down to achieve that.

This realization became a turning point. It became glaringly clear that I should concentrate, not on the harsh surface words, but on the deeper, underlying message. *Focusing beyond the surface* became my superpower. It's so easy to get caught up in the immediate reaction, the sharp tone, or the seemingly critical remark. But I learned that these are often just symptoms, not the root cause. When someone is lashing out, it's not about *me*; it's about *them* and their interpretation of the situation. It's about their fear, their insecurity, their past hurts, or their own unmet needs. By training myself to look past the initial presentation, I could begin to discern the true intent or the underlying pain.

This practice of seeing beyond the superficial allowed me to detach from emotional reactivity. Instead of feeling personally attacked, I could feel empathy. Instead of becoming defensive, I could become curious. This subtle but profound shift transformed my interactions. I realized that responding to the surface only perpetuates the cycle of frustration. By seeking the deeper message, I could address the true issue or, at the very least, avoid getting entangled in unnecessary conflict. This allowed me to choose peace, even when confronted with what appeared to be hostility.

So, when my mom or anyone else expressed themselves in a seemingly harsh or negative way, my internal question shifted to: "*Where is this coming from?*" This simple inquiry transformed my perspective entirely. It brought me to the liberating decision to not take things personally. This broadened my perspective, allowing me to step back from emotional reactivity. This change in how I processed the world culminated in asking myself the question that has been the cornerstone of my journey to peace, joy, and the experience of love: *"What in the big picture is really important?"* This question acts as my internal compass, guiding me away from petty grievances and toward what truly matters, and ensuring my energy is spent on constructive, rather than destructive, thoughts and actions.

This profound shift in focus, particularly the habit of asking, "What in the big picture is really important?" has helped me tremendously in my chosen profession: being a holistic dentist. It might seem like an unusual connection, but the parallels are undeniable. Every single day, I encounter multiple patients who are so consumed by fear of the dentist that they've neglected their teeth, often for years. As a direct consequence, their oral health, and frequently their systemic health, suffers significantly. This pervasive anxiety doesn't just manifest as missed appointments; it can lead to tangible physical symptoms like trembling hands, rapid heartbeats, sweaty palms, and even a tendency to lash out verbally or make dismissive comments. Patients might postpone critical treatments, leading to painful infections, lost teeth, and chronic discomfort that impacts their eating, speaking, and overall quality of life. Because of this intense fear, patients often don't express themselves in a kind or loving way. They might be irritable, defensive, or even outright hostile, simply because their anxiety levels are through the roof. But thanks to my early training in *focusing beyond the surface*, I am still able to treat them from a genuinely caring and nurturing place. I understand that their outward behavior is a symptom of their inner turmoil, not a personal affront.

My dental office isn't just a clinical space; I strive to make it a haven where patients feel heard and understood, not judged. This involves active listening, taking time to explain every step of a procedure in simple terms, using gentle language, and often, just allowing them to voice their fears without interruption. I might offer comfort measures like blankets or music, anything to create an atmosphere of calm. It's about building trust, one gentle word and one careful movement at a time. I have been very successful at guiding them to the realization that a dental visit doesn't have to be a stressful or anxious experience. This is, in fact, the very reason I became a dentist in the first place. My initial motivation wasn't just about fixing teeth; it was about healing fear and restoring confidence. I knew the power of a healthy smile, not just aesthetically, but emotionally.

There is nothing more gratifying than witnessing a patient, who once trembled in the waiting room, gradually relax, participate in their treatment, and ultimately break through their deeply ingrained fear. When they sit up after a procedure, often with tears of relief or a surprised smile, and say, "That wasn't nearly as bad as I thought!" Well, that's the moment of profound gratification. It's not just about the tooth I fixed; it's about the emotional barrier they shattered, the internal victory they achieved. This is the essence of my daily work: helping people reclaim their oral health and, in doing so, reclaiming a piece of peace and self-assurance. It's a privilege to facilitate that transformation.

Setbacks

I, like so many, have had obstacles to overcome to live my dream, setbacks that have become my comeback story. It's almost unbelievable, but I very nearly didn't make it through dental school. My journey was dramatically interrupted six months prior to graduating from Boston University Dental School. I was walking home from school, just like any other day, deep in thought, crossing Mass Avenue. Suddenly, a car, oblivious to the traffic laws, ran through a red light and struck me as I was in the crosswalk. The impact was violent and jarring. I remember the sickening crunch, the sensation of flying, completely disoriented, before landing hard on the asphalt near the sidewalk. The shock that coursed through my body was immense, momentarily dulling the pain. When I finally gathered myself enough to look down, my stomach dropped. My right leg was grotesquely broken, my foot pointing in the opposite direction, an image that remains seared into my memory. I was rushed to the hospital, where the full reality of the injury set in. I underwent emergency surgery to place a long internal nail in my shin, a permanent reminder of that day.

The physical pain in the weeks and months that followed was relentless, a constant companion that tested every fiber of my being. Beyond the pain, the frustration of immobility was crushing. Learning to navigate life with crutches, then a walker, and slowly, painstakingly, putting one foot in front of the other to regain my ability to walk unaided was a grueling process that stretched for about a year. My dental career, which felt so close, had to be put on an indefinite hold.

That year was without a doubt one of the toughest of my life. Unable to attend school, I had to find a way to support myself. With my right leg out of commission, I learned to drive using only my left leg and took a job as a pizza delivery person. Imagine the logistical challenges of delivering pizzas with a fractured leg! But I was determined. I slowly worked my way up to being a manager at the pizza place and took on security guard jobs during the night to make ends meet. The hours were long, the work was physically demanding, even for someone fully recovered, and the emotional toll of seeing my dreams deferred was immense. Yet, through all the pain, the exhaustion, and the uncertainty, I never once doubted that I would return to school. This unwavering conviction was sustained by my focus on the bigger picture: The dream of becoming a dentist, of helping others, was too strong to be extinguished by a temporary setback.

After that challenging year, I finally met with the school administration to devise a re-entry plan. To my dismay, they informed me that due to the length of my absence and the curriculum changes, I would have to take another two years of school before I could graduate. Two more years after already being so close! It was a blow, but I didn't let it derail me. Instead, it became a moment of profound clarity. This setback wasn't a wall; it was a detour that ultimately deepened my resolve. I had a choice: Succumb to despair and abandon my dream or harness the challenge as a forge for my inner strength. I chose the latter.

The entire time I was focused on that guiding light, that big picture. I vividly remember the quiet moments of reflection, visualizing myself in a dental operation, not just fixing teeth, but truly connecting with patients, easing their fears, and witnessing their transformation. This wasn't merely about completing a degree; it was about embodying a purpose. I saw beyond the immediate pain and inconvenience of my injury and the added years of schooling, focusing instead on the immense satisfaction I knew I would derive from helping others overcome their anxieties and discover their own inherent worth through a healthy smile.

Empowering Others

The vision of empowering individuals—showing them that the limiting beliefs they held about themselves, their fears, their anxieties were simply not the truth—became my unwavering beacon. The thought of witnessing that shift in their demeanor, the newfound confidence radiating from them, and the sheer joy of knowing they had conquered something within themselves that had caused such chaos and neglect in their lives were nothing short of miraculous. That powerful vision fueled every single step of those additional two years, transforming what could have been a crushing defeat into a period of profound growth and unwavering dedication to my goal.

One of my absolute favorite examples, one that truly embodies the power of transformation that I strive for in my practice, involved a good-looking, yet noticeably overweight, tall African American teenager who first came to my office. He presented with spotted white and uneven front teeth, a clear source of self-consciousness, compounded by significant anxiety about being at the dentist's office. His initial demeanor was very withdrawn; he kept his head down, mumbled his responses, and avoided eye contact. His mom brought him to me, not for cosmetic work, but for a regular checkup, simply because I accepted their very basic insurance. I could tell immediately that, beyond the physical dental issues, there was an emotional weight to his smile. In a nurturing and caring way, I slowly built rapport with him and his mom. I focused on making each visit comfortable, explaining every step, and celebrating small victories.

Over a few appointments, I was able to get him to complete some necessary fillings and cleanings. But I always noticed that when I spoke to him directly, he would constantly look down as if ashamed of his smile. One day, his mom pulled me aside, her voice laced with concern. She confided that in just a few months, his high school prom would take place, and he felt so profoundly ashamed of his smile that he couldn't bring himself to ask anyone and therefore had no girlfriend for the event. She knew their insurance wouldn't cover anything "nice" cosmetically, but since he had become comfortable with me, she desperately asked for my help, hoping for a solution that might restore his confidence. My heart went out to them. This was exactly why I became a dentist, not just to fix teeth, but to address the underlying emotional pain.

In the next few weeks, working within their means, I was able to place naturally white crowns on his front teeth. The change was immediate and dramatic. When he saw his new smile in the mirror for the first time, a slow, incredulous grin spread across his face. It wasn't just his teeth that changed; his entire expression shifted. Soon after, he and his mom came to see me with some truly exciting news. Beaming, they showed me a picture of him and his new girlfriend, whom he was proudly taking to prom! He was absolutely bursting with confidence and joy, a palpable result of conquering his anxiety and embracing his new self-perception. He had finally realized that he was so much more than he had given himself credit for.

We lost touch for a couple of years due to changes in his insurance, as often happens. But then, one day, he walked back into my office, and I was genuinely blown away. He was now a tall, slim, incredibly handsome young man. The transformation was not just physical; he exuded an aura of confidence and self-love that was truly inspiring. And if that wasn't enough, when I asked him what he did for work, he looked me straight in the eye with a broad, confident smile and said, "I'm a model!" It was a moment of profound validation for both of us. His journey from a shy, anxious teenager hiding his smile to a confident young man embracing his full potential was a powerful testament to the impact of addressing both physical and emotional needs. This case exemplifies the core of my purpose as a dentist: to help individuals see their inherent worth and step into their best selves.

Your choices become your truth. The teenager's story is a beautiful illustration of how, sometimes, individuals need some sort of outside validation to truly absorb the fact that they are whole and perfect just as they are. Society often conditions you to seek external approval, to believe that your worth is dictated by others' opinions or by superficial standards. You are bombarded with images and messages that whisper, "You're not good enough." The profound truth is this: You are all unique and beautiful. You possess an inherent worth that requires no external validation. So, why do you carry around all these misconceptions about yourself, these limiting beliefs, and call them the truth? Why do you allow these self-imposed narratives to define your potential and diminish your own joy?

How incredibly freeing it is to understand that you choose who you are and how you see the world. This isn't just a feel-good platitude; it's a fundamental principle of psychological freedom. When you truly grasp that your perspective is your power, a vast landscape of possibility opens before you. For me, I have been blessed to understand early in life that my opinion of myself is the only one that truly matters. This conviction didn't come overnight; it was forged through years of observation, self-reflection, and conscious practice, just like the heroes in my childhood books taught me.

The wisdom I've gained from navigating life's unpredictable currents, from observing my mother's struggles, from my own physical setback, and from helping countless patients overcome their fears has indelibly shaped my understanding of worthiness. True worthiness isn't something granted by others or earned through accomplishments; it's an intrinsic state, a recognition of your inherent value that comes from within. This wisdom allows me to filter all external input through the lens of my own self-worth. If someone's words or actions don't align with my understanding of my own inherent value, I can choose to let them go, understanding that their perspective does not define my truth. This is the ultimate freedom that comes from lived experience and the conscious application of its lessons.

The fact is that *you* get to say who *you* are and what *you* focus on; it's *your* choice. Are you focusing on perceived flaws, past mistakes, or external judgments? Or are you choosing to focus on your strengths, your resilience, and your inherent beauty? Like I said in the beginning, what you feed your mind, what you tell yourself, and what you ultimately believe is entirely up to you. This is the ultimate freedom, and it requires conscious effort. It's about cultivating a positive inner dialogue, actively challenging those negative thoughts that whisper doubts in your mind. Start today. Keep reminding yourself how amazing you are, how smart you are, how beautiful you are. Affirm your capabilities, celebrate your small victories, and acknowledge your unique talents. When a challenging thought arises, ask yourself, "*Do I choose to accept this? Is this serving me?*" and then consciously choose a thought that lifts you up. With so many ways to view something, so many narratives you can adopt about yourself and the world around you, why not choose the one that empowers you the most, the one that ignites your peace, joy, and the boundless experience of love? The power is within you.

REFLECTIONS FOR YOU?

- Are the thoughts you are feeding your mind making you stressed or giving you peace and joy?

- How can you change your thinking about something that stresses you to bring you peace and joy instead?

- What language are you using with yourself and about yourself that makes you feel less powerful or confident?

- How can you speak to yourself and about yourself to help you feel empowered and more confident?

Connect with Dr. Steven:

What "THE GRASS GROWS WHERE I AM" Means to Me

> I truly know and believe I am a winner on every level and that the grass is green wherever I choose to water it, rather than perceiving that it's greener 'on the other side.'

Diana Drake

Connect with Diana:

Thyroid & Hormone Healing Power: Wisdom Gained with Homeopathy and Natural Herb Protocols

Diana M. Drake, PhD

Great minds discuss ideas; average minds discuss events; small minds discuss people.

—Eleanor Roosevelt

Have you ever felt that your body is betraying you as you are aging? Are you tired of being told that you need drugs for health concerns, but you're never told the root cause of your issues? My goal for the readers at the end of this chapter is to understand that there is a REASON for dysfunction at all ages. I work to naturally balance hormones, skin, and thyroid issues, which are my specialties as a naturopathic practitioner. I am also a homeopathic medicine manufacturer.

My name is Diana Drake and my passion for natural medicine began when I lost my mother to her second heart attack when she was fifty-three and I was twenty-three, but let's rewind first. My mother suffered her first heart attack when I was only seven years old.

I remember how shocking the news was. She was young, beautiful, and in great shape. It was determined by the doctors that her cholesterol was too high and that was likely the cause of her cardiovascular event. She began a statin drug when she was thirty-two. A few years later it was recommended that I get tested for cholesterol because the doctors suspected this was genetic. Sure enough, my cholesterol level was almost 600 and I was also put on a statin drug. At the time I was in fifth grade. I began to suffer from horrible body aches and pains on this drug, but my cholesterol was now "in range" at around 200.

Just twenty years later my mother passed peacefully in her sleep from her second heart attack. After this devastating news sank in, I began to wonder in the weeks that followed, "How did this happen if her cholesterol was in range?" This was soon followed by, "Could I end up dying too?" Was this drug PROTECTING ME? This was when I first realized there was something very wrong with Western medicine. I spent the next few years of my life learning the root causes for cardiovascular issues and how to support overall cardiovascular and circulatory system health. I also worked with an incredible naturopath who got me off the statin drugs and successfully had me balanced properly with natural supplements.

Here is the spoiler alert: Heart disease is not caused by a deficiency in cholesterol medication. This is a concept that I will explain to each new client. There is a root cause, and it is my job to uncover that cause. When the cause is found, the body is best brought back into balance using nutrition, homeopathy, and herbal supplements that help us reach homeostasis rather than a drug that simply acts as a band aid, and a dangerous one at that. There is not one single drug on the market today that does not have risks and side effects that often lead to a cascade of health decline that requires more drugs. It was this life event of losing my mother that brought me on the journey I find myself on today. It was gaining *wisdom* through this loss that set a new intention of becoming a naturopath myself. At the time I was an esthetician and saw my business blending beautifully to become a holistic haven for skin issues, cardiovascular issues, and women's health.

Dr. Theresa Dale

During my first year as a newly graduated naturopath, I heard Dr. Theresa Dale speaking about hormone and thyroid issues at a convention. Not only did she have a deep understanding of this space, but her company manufactured homeopathic hormone and thyroid products and protocols. Her protocols had a focus on removing the root cause, proper testing using saliva instead of blood, and implementing remedies to restore proper native function to the body. Though I found the endocrine system to be a complex space that I was not familiar with, her philosophy and products deeply resonated with me.

I opened my practice shortly thereafter and to my surprise I was flooded with people who needed help with hormones and thyroid issues yet showed little interest in the cardiovascular realm. I knew that I had to pivot and get an understanding of these concepts to properly serve the women who had sought me out. I was so blessed to become one of Dr. Theresa Dale's last disciples. I studied under her for five years before she suddenly passed away in 2022. Sadly, she didn't let any of us know she was sick, so her patients and practitioners alike were left shocked. To this news, my first thought was, what is going to happen to this incredible, one-of-a-kind, medicine? There were hundreds of naturopaths and customers across the country, including myself, who relied on her medicines as crucial tools for our clients. I immediately spoke to her family, who had inherited her company, and I was able to acquire the business.

Now, through this work, her legacy can live on. It has become my sole mission to educate the community that there are alternative health options to drugs and hormone therapy! There is always a natural course to pursue before resorting to a pharmaceutical product. Now at this point, you absolutely must be wondering, is it possible to restore hormone health without the use of actual hormones? Following are some facts and history that will bring clarity to this question:

The Homeopathic Hormone Rejuvenation System (created by Dr. Theresa Dale) is designed to balance hormones using nontoxic homeopathic remedies rather than natural or synthetic hormone replacement. Recent evidence in medical literature has brought to our attention the side effects of synthetic hormone replacement. Even "natural" hormone replacement can cause significant symptoms, including abnormal and toxic hormone levels and liver congestion. Findings from the Women's Health Initiative Memory Study (WHIMS) published in the May 28, 2003, issue of the *Journal of the American Medical Association* have highlighted a downside to combination hormone replacement therapy (HRT) in postmenopausal women. Researchers from Wake Forest University Baptist Medical Center found that the combination of estrogen plus progestin is associated with *double the rate of dementia* in women sixty-five years of age and older who took the hormones for an average of four years compared to those not on HRT. HRT, whether natural or synthetic, is based on the incorrect assumption that your body becomes incapable of producing appropriate hormones simply because you have reached a certain age. Yes, your body does alter its hormone production as you pass through the stages of your life, but hormone levels are an indicator of how healthy you are, not how old you are.

Natural hormone usage has grown since synthetic HRT has been deemed toxic and a potential cancer risk. Millions of women are now using synthetic, natural "plant-derived" and synthesized "bioidentical" hormones. The problem for the consumer is education about product safety. Natural progesterone, estrogen, and wild yam creams can cause an extreme toxicity in hormone levels. If a woman's progesterone level is 100 and it jumps to 6,500 due to use of a cream, this becomes a toxic burden to the liver and immune system. Ninety percent of women using "natural" and or compounded progesterone or estrogens from wild yam (soy) for more than three months have elevated toxic levels, abnormal hormone ratios and cortisol levels, and/or hormonal toxicity (overly increased hormone levels that burden the liver and immune system). Ninety-five percent of women using HRT synthetic progesterone and estrogen have abnormal hormone ratios, estrogen dominance, abnormal cortisol levels, and toxicity. One hundred percent of women on synthetic hormones risk cancer. Toxic levels of synthetic hormones may take longer to indicate on serum (blood tests), as well as saliva.

One thousand before and after saliva tests by Dr Theresa Dale, taken on women using the homeopathic hormone rejuvenation system, show NO TOXICITY. Clinical testing reveals astounding results, including testing on women with a complete hysterectomy. Once the ovaries are removed, the body can convert hormone production to the adrenals. On a group of one thousand women with hysterectomies who were tested before and after using a saliva test, 100 percent of women showed that their adrenal glands are making the needed hormones for their body and 95 percent of their symptoms had abated.

What exactly is homeopathy and how is it used to create a hormone system?

Homeopathy is a therapy developed by Dr. Samuel Hahnemann in Germany over two hundred years ago. It is currently the second largest system of medicine in the world. It is a form of energy medicine in which each remedy is very diluted. Remedies are derived from many of the original materials including botanicals, animal organs and glands, minerals, bacteria, chemicals, viruses, radiation, disease, poisons, and hormones. Very little, if any, of the original substance remains in a homeopathic remedy because it has been diluted so many times that only the imprint or "frequency" of the original substance remains. This frequency is used in the body as a remedy. Sarcodes are a particular type of homeopathic remedy. They are made from healthy tissue and organs. They bring the specific organ back to correct function. The Dr. Dale Homeopathic Hormone Rejuvenation system contains both sarcodes and classical remedies. Only the energy of the material remains because of the level of dilution. It is important to note if you are considering this for yourself that caffeine, mint, synthetic fragrance, exposure to X-Rays, and radiation must be 100 percent avoided while taking homeopathy. This is because these interfere with the frequency of the medicines.

Conventional Versus Advanced

Homeopathic Approach to Healing

Unfortunately, the entire Western medical system is a for-profit business. This system is built on sick care—NOT healthcare, wellness, or any sort of prevention. The current Western medical model will never allow for flourishing health because its primary function is to profit from illness. From diagnostics to drugs, surgery, vaccines, and hospital stays. It's a nearly 5 trillion dollar per year industry, and for it to keep working, patients must stay IN the system. To be truly well and balanced means you are not a part of the system and therefore cannot turn a profit for it. Let's have a look at an overview of conventional versus homeopathic/naturopathic medicine.

Conventional:

- Treats only the symptoms
- Suppresses disease and the immune system
- Creates side effects
- Creates toxicity
- Causes the body to become addicted to hormones
- Treatment is based on diagnosis and classical symptoms with some individualization
- A centralized, connected, for-profit system linked with insurance companies that have quotas and profitability requirements

Homeopathic/Naturopathic:

- Addresses symptoms and individual sensitivity
- Locates and heals at the root cause
- Balances through broad spectrum capabilities
- Has no side effects
- Has/causes no toxicity
- Decentralized, no insurance, no profitability requirements

Homeopathy & Hormone Rejuvenation

Homeopathic remedies can improve progesterone uptake and metabolism. They do not interfere with the normal shift from progesterone dominance to estrogen dominance during the month. Another fascinating factor in healing hormonal conditions with homeopathy is that homeopathic protocols do not have any side effects because they contain only minute amounts of substances. Even though there are only trace amounts of therapeutic ingredients in homeopathy, clinical experience with these medicines shows that the infinitesimal doses they offer work on unconscious people, infants, and animals and are therefore not a placebo.

Dr. Dale's hormone remedies can be utilized effectively for hormone rejuvenation by stimulating production of natural hormones in the human body. The homeopathic substances that are used to balance endocrine and hormonal symptoms are currently sourced from botanical and mineral substances in addition to healthy tissue or secretions of the body, such as hormones. Examples of homeopathic ingredients include Chelidonium, which can address liver congestion, Sepia for hot flashes and sulfur for delayed menses and hot flashes. Dr. Dale's topical and sublingual remedies can stimulate a healing response in the targeted organ, thus stimulating the normal functionality of that organ.

Homeopathy is nonaddictive, and it does not replace any innate function of the body. It truly helps with healing the body, mind, and spirit. And unlike other medicine types, as you begin to feel better, the dosage can be lowered. We do not repopulate, we repair! It's difficult for people to grasp this concept, but flooding the body with its missing hormones only creates more confusion and does not address the root cause of the wrench in the system. It also atrophies your body's ability to properly make its own hormones. Homeopathic hormone rejuvenation is a holistic system that includes the frequencies of your entire endocrine system. It is an energetic medicine kit that is balancing and repairing on a cellular level without any negative side effects. I'll say that again, there are NO NEGATIVE or DANGEROUS side effects when you use homeopathic remedies. And because the kit is balancing on the endocrine system, you can use it on any hormonal situation, regardless of your specific hormone profile.

Another incredible issue is thyroid dysfunction in women. Levothyroxine is reaching the No. 1 most prescribed drug in the United States. Taking into consideration my previous points, what happens if we simply give the body more thyroid hormones? Yes, thyroid-stimulating hormone (TSH) will come into balance in the labs, which will make your doctor happy, and you will feel okay for a while. Then as time goes on, your thyroid may atrophy and stop producing hormones all together. Whatever root cause that knocked your thyroid out in the first place will continue to rage on in your body unchecked, which may eventually bring your symptoms back regardless of your TSH numbers. Did you know that your thyroid is supposed to be made up of 60 percent iodine? Yet 95 percent of my thyroid patients test for iodine deficiency and bromine dominance. This means that the thyroid is full of toxic potassium bromine in the receptor sites rather than iodine. What is potassium bromide? A chemical used in pool/hot tub sanitizers, pesticides, and fire-retardant chemicals sprayed on sofas, mattresses, furniture, carpets, and drapes. It is also added to US bleached flour, making this toxic chemical pretty much impossible to avoid.

Your thyroid also needs other elements, including selenium and zinc, to do its job. However, this sensitive little gland gets junked up with bromine, heavy metals, glyphosate, chlorine, and so on. Yet doctors are not checking for any of these biomarkers when evaluating our thyroids. When elevated thyroid peroxidase (TPO) antibodies come back, this is the body showing an immune response in the thyroid as well. As a naturopath I do not subscribe to the "auto-immune" theory that the body attacks itself for no reason. There is always a reason. A hypo-thyroid condition with an auto-immune response is a serious endocrine and immune imbalance that takes a lot more than a TSH pill to fix. Since there is no drug for Hashimoto's (elevated TPO) doctors are rarely even testing for this anymore unless you see a specialist or have a practitioner who is more aware. On top of the recommendations for drugs, doctors do not offer any lifestyle or diet advice for these conditions. Not because they are too lazy, but simply because their lack of education in this matter makes them ignorant of nutrition. Nutrition is the foundation of our cellular health. If you are working with ANYONE who does not understand this, please seek someone who does.

Proper thyroid screening should include TSH, TPO, T3, T4, iodine, selenium, bromine and a heavy metal panel. Saliva hormones and a full cortisol day map should also be included to thoroughly assess your endocrine health. If you are NOT getting this, I encourage you to find a practitioner who works this way. Lastly, I want to mention polycystic ovary syndrome (PCOS). Something I am finding in MOST women and grossly misdiagnosed by Western medicine. If you have the following symptoms, PLEASE PROPERLY check for PCOS:

- Ovarian cysts
- Elevated androstenedione levels
- Elevated DHEA levels
- Blood sugar imbalance
- Stubborn belly fat

- Painful periods (more than 3 out of 10 pain level or bad enough to take a pain reliever)
- Dark facial hair
- Abnormal cycles/skipping periods
- Trouble conceiving or carrying to full term
- Acne

Please understand that although PCOS stands for polycystic ovarian syndrome, not all women will have cysts on the ovaries. Therefore, a pelvic ultrasound is NOT enough data to tell a woman that she doesn't have PCOS. The proper diagnostic for this syndrome is to check androstenedione levels—everyone with PCOS will have this elevated. Just like other hormones, it is best to check this via saliva. PCOS is typically an indicator of insulin resistance caused by a diet too high in sugar, processed grains, and seed oils—which is 75 percent of the standard American diet. If you have PCOS, there are great diet changes you can make and PCOS is very well managed with the proper supplements. Please *DO NOT* get on birth control for periods and/or acne regulation! If you are or have a teenager who has skin issues, painful periods, or abnormal periods, please work with someone who will get to the root of the issues rather than just recommend birth control, spironolactone, antibiotics, or Accutane. PCOS is also referred to as "diabetes of the ovaries" and it is a metabolic condition that causes a lot of issues in females.

I truly hope I have awakened something in you to encourage you to continue down this path. If you are currently on a drug for your hormones, skin, thyroid, or other reasons and would like to look at other options, I happily invite you to reach out to me as I work virtually with clients across the United States. I am also diligently training other practitioners on how to assess hormone health and build protocols using homeopathic and herbal medicine. My goal in this lifetime is to help as many people as possible and to awaken you to the understanding that health is your birthright. Drugs are not health; they are simply symptom management. Real health takes real work to overcome the increasing toxicity in our environment and decreasing nutrients in our soil and food supply. It is time to water the grass and become your own health advocate so that the grass can continue to grow, where you are.

Reflections for You

- Do you believe the human body is designed to produce its own hormones from birth to death?

- Do you support big pharma and trust them with your health?

- Do you believe in your body's ability to heal itself?

- Do you accept that we age and embrace these natural changes? Or do you fear them?

- How can you nurture your aging process in a holistic way?

What "THE GRASS GROWS WHERE I AM" Means to Me

> That the challenges I experience are specifically for me so I can grow and become an even better version of me. By accepting my challenges and nurturing my gifts I create a fertile grass and continue to step into the woman I am meant to be.

Ester Mizrahi

Connect with Ester:

The Wisdom of Nonnegotiables

Ester Mizrahi

We don't have to fulfill ALL our dreams, but we do need to recognize which ones are our true mission in life.

Growing up I experienced a myriad of challenges that led me to self-doubt with unhealthy habits. As a very social teen I experienced a lot of success, and when I finally experienced rejection, it led to a lack of self-worth. This unfamiliar territory turned rejection into a crushing heartbreak. To ease the pain and fuel the search for adrenaline and mystery, I turned to smoking and drinking with friends, desperately looking for something. This introduced me to the infamous munchies that go along with the side effects of weed and hashish, as do laziness and lack of motivation. Not only did it drive me further away from my search for happiness and excitement, but also slowly but surely, I started to gain weight. It just snuck up on me when I wasn't paying attention. Now, every time I was rejected, I blamed it on my weight. It became my excuse for rejection and failure.

On top of that, my home environment was not helping my unease at being overweight. My mother would simultaneously encourage me to lose weight while feeding me delicious food. How confusing! It even got to the point that when she would hide the candies in the house, my brothers and I would search until we found them. I became increasingly frustrated by the realization that I was rounder than most of my twiggy friends. Many of them starved themselves or resorted to vomiting to stay thin. Thankfully, I knew that was not for me. I was so unhappy, which created in me an immense desire to be skinny. In my quest for answers, I turned to my grandmothers for advice. One suggested drinking apple cider vinegar while the other told me to eat something I liked until I got sick of it, which didn't work because I still love chocolate to this day!

One day a person I admired told me a very impactful story about the health challenges she had. She shared with me that she was told by doctors that she would die due to certain health conditions if she did not change her diet dramatically. She was informed by a nutritional doctor that a strict plant-based diet was her only hope to live. In the 1960s, the term "vegan" was a very weird concept, something that did not even make sense in the early sixties to many. She had no other option, so despite the diet's reputation, she committed to it. That nonnegotiable decision not only saved her life but also made her healthier and more energetic than many women her own age. Today at seventy-seven years old, she is vibrant, healthy, and beautiful with kids and grandkids.

Her example of commitment to her health sparked in me a passion for my own health. If she could turn her health around, then why couldn't I? In the beginning I had not made it a nonnegotiable for myself. I bounced between a sedentary lifestyle and partying. It was a constant back-and-forth, from being a party girl to a gym rat. The cycle continued until I became a mother, which requires energy. Being a mom is a role that inspired my passion and obsession with health. I finally had the motivation I needed to solidify my pursuit for my own excellent health. I officially became a fitness trainer and left my nightlife behind. My journey into fitness and health began when I discovered a love of cardio, dancing, running, and spinning as effective ways to lose weight.

The Importance of Spiritual Practice

I also realized the importance of spiritual practice. Through my spiritual studies, I've learned that we are all here to work on ourselves. Years ago, I developed the spiritual habit of observing Shabbat (the Jewish day of rest). On this holy day, I refrain from driving or using electronics; it's a holy day for me. And I organize my life around it. To honor this day, I established the habit of going to the ocean on Fridays, regardless of the weather. Rain or shine, stormy or calm, I make it a point to immerse myself in the ocean water. However, every single time I arrive at the beach, a voice in my head tells me, "It's too cold. It's dangerous. Maybe not today because I may not be in the mood." Yet I never let that voice win; I always enter the water. And once I'm in, I'm okay. By putting myself on autopilot and ignoring those negative thoughts, I emerge victorious. If I were to personify that little voice in my head, it would resemble a small, defeated woman, sitting on the sidelines in judgment, knowing she's lost. Meanwhile, the confident version of me stands tall, grinning, reminding myself of my victory.

Life presents us with various situations, big and small, and our strength often lies in our perspective. Whether it is our mental or physical health, we all have stories we tell ourselves about our life experiences. Yes, we encounter successes, but we also face failures. I believe that it is through those failures we can learn the most.

Ultimately, it's your decision whether to move forward or dwell on your past. If you choose to look back, you may get stuck. I often compare life to the ocean, as it is sometimes calm, but sometimes it's tumultuous. The wise learn to navigate the waves, and those who surf embrace the challenges. We even learn to enjoy the challenges. We all have solutions and the right decisions available to us. The moment you declare something nonnegotiable, you win.

Making Better Lifestyle Choices

People consult with me in my coaching practice to help them improve their mindset and make better lifestyle choices to improve their health, energy, and sleep, and reduce their stress and worries. Often, all it takes is a single nonnegotiable decision to start changing their life. This is my daily mission: to identify that one thing that can enhance your life by helping you foster a deep awareness and strength. Initially, embracing this change can be challenging, especially after experiencing failure before. However, once you succeed, you'll learn to celebrate life and win on repeat. Knowledge is vital but implementing it is when your life truly changes. Learning to remove the negative lingering voices in your head, to minimize their power over you is crucial for your success. Also do not fall into the trap of following the crowd or doing things simply because others do it.

Remind yourself of your goals and do not use every celebration as an opportunity to indulge. For example, I once attended a networking event where I was surrounded by delicious food. I reminded myself that I came there to connect with others and not just to eat. I can eat at home where I can choose more mindfully what I eat without guilt.

Cultivating a strong mindset is a shift you can make to stay in charge and in control of your daily choices. Don't wait till it's too late to adopt a healthier lifestyle. For example, bodybuilders adhere to a strict diet simply because they have a goal in mind. Their choices and decisions become nonnegotiable, and they refrain from momentary pleasures that jeopardize their long-term success.

Declare non-negotiables. End the overthinking. Consistency becomes identity and you win on repeat.

Most individuals in Western countries often tell themselves, "Tomorrow, I will eat healthier." Often, it takes a health scare or a body image crisis for people to wake up. Parents, too, often resort to quick, unhealthy options, such as french fries or pizza, for their children, believing it's easier than preparing healthy meals. When I ask why they chose these options, they often reply that their kids are "*picky eaters.*" My retort is simple: "Who made them picky?" I don't believe in discussing weight with children, nor do I think we should ignore food conversations altogether. Educating children about healthy options, like the benefits of fruits and vegetables, is crucial. It's more dangerous for our kids to develop weight issues or eating disorders when they consume unhealthy foods. Parents should be mindful of what they introduce to their children from an early age, so they won't have these problems later in life.

As a busy fitness trainer and coach, I initially believed it didn't matter how I obtained my protein, whether through shakes, powders, or animal sources. However, as I matured, I realized that we often eat out of boredom or for temporary pleasure rather than for necessity. By listening to my inner voice and the dialogue within my mind, I began making nonnegotiable decisions about my diet.

To my surprise, a rash I had on and off since I was pregnant with my daughter . . . cleared up almost fifteen years later, once I adopted a healthy vegetarian lifestyle. This decision not only improved my health but also garnered compliments on my skin. I turned aging into a strength; I was determined to become stronger and more confident as I grew older.

Our Thoughts Shape Our Lives

My fascination with how our thoughts shape our lives led me to delve deeper into the psychology of our habits. After becoming a certified coach and learning techniques like Neuro-Linguistic Programming (NLP), I discovered how to control my mindset for better mental and physical health. My experience with my many clients and their stories made me understand people's minds and struggles; I realize that there is no big or small problem—it's in the client's eyes how big or small it is. I have implemented programs for my clients like these:

- **Facilitate Personalized Strategies:** I help my clients with their specific needs, wants, values, and goals. I help them build their action plans. I use techniques like goal-setting with well-formed outcomes to ensure plans are specific, measurable, achievable, relevant, and timebound.

- **Address Limiting Beliefs:** I use NLP techniques like reframing and belief change to help my clients identify and overcome limiting beliefs that are holding them back. For example, if a client says something negative, I use reframing to help them shift their perspective. In this way, I assist them in uncovering and realizing their specific spiritual power.

- **Focus on Empowerment and Self-Efficacy:** I empower clients to take ownership of their health and well-being. I celebrate their successes and help them learn from their specific challenges. For example:
  - *Clean Living:* I help clients identify their personal "toxin triggers" and help them create a customized plan for reducing exposure.
  - *Empowered Minds:* I help clients find a meditation technique that works for them to create consistent practice. I also help them understand their own internal dialogue and change unhelpful patterns.
  - *Transform Health:* I help clients discover their preferred forms of exercise and create a sustainable fitness routine. I help them understand their own internal representations of health and help them create more compelling representations.

In essence, as a certified coach and fitness trainer using NLP, I move beyond information delivery to:

- Facilitate lasting change.
- Empower clients to create their own solutions.
- Help clients tap into their inner resources.
- Help clients create powerful change.

We don't have to get sick to remember to adopt a healthy lifestyle. Let's choose healthy habits so we won't spend our time being sick.

I employ tools to manage worries and continue enjoying life without too many distractions. As I work together with my clients, I am amazed at how their awareness simplifies their life. I notice that when they succumb to negative thinking, they suffer during their workouts. Conversely, when they connect to positive thoughts, they feel lighter and freer. When it comes to food and fun, our bad habits can creep up on us so it's important to be mindful and present to them. This is why making nonnegotiable decisions is essential for our success. If you slip up, just remind yourself that you are human and don't beat yourself up. Learn to enjoy your journey and to learn from your mistakes. The power and connection between mindset and nutrition is profound, extending far beyond simply knowing what foods are healthy but also if they are right for you. In essence, mindset is the invisible force that shapes your relationship with your food and everything you do. By cultivating a positive and empowering mindset with a few nonnegotiables, you can reach your goals and have the lasting change you desire.

It's also about the psychological framework that shapes your eating habits, influencing everything from your food choices to your overall relationship with food. Helping people change their lives through awareness has become my passion and purpose. Cultivating awareness from the moment you wake up and throughout your day is important for a multitude of reasons, impacting everything from your physical and mental health to your relationships and overall well-being. Awareness allows you to recognize and acknowledge your emotions as they arise rather than react impulsively in the moment. Awareness helps you manage stress, anxiety, and other challenging emotions more effectively. You can identify triggers and therefore choose how you respond to them. Awareness provides clarity and focus, enabling you to make more informed and thoughtful decisions. You become less susceptible to impulsive choices driven by emotions or external pressures.

By understanding your internal state, you can make decisions that align with your values and goals. Awareness fosters a deeper understanding of your thoughts, feelings, and behaviors. This self-knowledge empowers you to identify patterns, strengths, and areas for growth. You become aware of your own internal dialogue, and therefore you can change it. Mindful awareness helps you stay present at this moment, reducing rumination on the past or worries about your future. This can significantly reduce your stress and anxiety levels. Awareness improves your ability to listen attentively and communicate effectively. You become more empathetic and compassionate, fostering stronger and more meaningful connections with others.

Wonder Woman

It was a hot day when I first started working with Dr. R. She was tall, very pretty, and successful. From the outside it looked like she had it all. She had an amazing family, a successful husband, a beautiful home, a great community, even the perfect car. But as we spoke, I quickly heard the things she truly needed: mindset, lifestyle, posture, and awareness. Her biggest struggle was her weight. She believed being overweight was her destiny because of family history and age. As a doctor and busy mother of five, she lived under constant stress and long hours, always giving to everyone else. She kept saying, "It's hard." That was the first shift we made—changing "hard" to "challenging." When you change the way you speak about your life, your life changes. We began with posture and awareness, not only in the way she stood but also in the way she ate and lived. I showed her how to slow down, breathe, be present and even chew with awareness.

I introduced her to short meditations. At first, she thought meditation was only for monks, but within minutes of sitting quietly, listening to my voice with soft music and the birds singing, she felt a peace she had never known. With just a few sessions, both in person and online, she began to sleep better, relax deeper, and see herself differently. She never misses a session and prefers twice a week, saying that in forty-five minutes she gets to open her heart, stretch, receive advice, and reset. Her husband and children tell me she has become a better mom and wife. She tells everyone I am her coach, therapist, trainer, and friend. To me, she is Wonder Woman, though she doesn't always see it. Her story reminds me that awareness and small changes can transform everything. Awareness of your body's signals allows you to make healthier choices regarding nutrition, exercise, and sleep. Mindful eating, for example, promotes better digestion and satiation. Awareness of your physical state allows you to react to pain or discomfort before it becomes a larger issue. Awareness cultivates a sense of gratitude and appreciation for the present moment. This will lead to a more fulfilling and joyful life.

Small, Consistent Changes

A story that has profoundly influenced my life is that of Rabbi Akiva, a sage who started from humble beginnings. He didn't know how to read or write until the age of forty. One day, he observed a drop of water consistently falling onto a rock, creating a hole. This realization illustrated how small, consistent efforts can lead to monumental change. Many clients express certainty that they will achieve their goals eventually but not right now. I remind them that there is never a perfect time to start. The best time to plant a tree was years ago; the second-best time is now. When people contemplate weight loss or improving their health, they often focus solely on workouts or diets. However, true transformation occurs in the mind.

In my classes, I emphasize that the hardest part of working out is simply showing up. This may require waking up earlier and sacrificing the pleasure of scrolling through your phone or TV. You need to ask yourself the right questions and visualize achieving your goals, along with the necessary steps to get there. If you neglect your mindset, you'll continue making excuses and justifying poor choices. This level of enlightenment is what will help you change your toxic coping methods and open you up to change. You will grow and show others by example how you can harness your inner wisdom and, in the moment of decision, come out victorious because you have lived, learned, and done better for yourself. I've encountered clients who proudly present their "perfect" food lists but conveniently forget about the small indulgences they allow themselves. Occasional cheats are often excused by claims of "it's just once in a while" or "it's a special occasion."

When people are too comfortable in their current situation, they may resist change, making it challenging for them to get the support they desire. Having commitment to yourself and taking small steps daily will lead to significant achievements, so you can develop your best self. Embrace small daily habits such as a morning routine that may include prayer, gratitude, movement, drinking water, and avoiding empty-calorie foods. I've discovered that small daily habits can make a tremendous difference in my clients' overall well-being. As I continue to guide my clients on their wellness journeys, I emphasize the importance of developing their identities as the architects of their thoughts. We should not merely be passengers; we need to take the lead and direct our minds toward success. Are you ready to empower your mindset and transform your health? Connect with me and let me help you become healthy and strong.

Remembering that there's a higher hand guiding your life is the moment control fades and trust begins.

Reflections for You

- What are your nonnegotiables?

- What fears have held you back from going after the life you truly desire?

- What dream do you regret not starting long ago—the dream you gave up on but still lives quietly inside you?

- What's something you see others doing that inspires you—something you wish you could make part of your life, but you keep putting off?

- If there's something you wish you'd started in the past or something you admire in others but haven't adopted yet, why haven't you done it?

Connect with Ester:

Acknowledgments

Thank you, G♥d, for your daily love and support, and especially for my beautiful family and for bringing Steven, my soulmate, into my life. I am forever grateful for the miracles I get to experience daily.

My deepest gratitude and love go out to each of the coauthors who participated in this book. Your patience, love, and dedication made this beautiful collaboration possible.

Thank you to Lisa Ray, who originated the idea for this anthology. Your support of me and our authors brought this book to life.

A heartfelt thank you to Patricia Neyra, my sister. Your contribution to our book design, organization, and lead funnels are beautiful and effective. We truly make a great team!

Thank you to The Book Couple, Gary and Carol Rosenberg, for your support in launching our book into the world. I love working with you both.

With deep gratitude to you, the reader, who chose to read and be inspired by the stories we have shared here. May you continue shining your light brightly every day and nurturing your greenest grass.

About the Anthologist

Noah Crane
#1 Bestselling Author and CEO

Noah Crane is the author of *The Grass Is Greenest Where I Am* and *The Love & Light Journal*. Noah is also a mindset coach, storyteller, the current president of the Holistic Chamber of Commerce, Boca Raton Chapter, and founder of the World Healing Tour, a movement devoted to remembering who we are and living a life full of purpose and passion.

As the creator of the 3G Effect mindset, she encourages us to practice three important elements daily to create more ease and flow in our lives. She designed the 3G Effect Jewelry Collection as a wearable reminder to have a grateful heart, to be grounded in love and compassion, and that you are guided by G♥d daily.

Rooted in her Israeli childhood and shaped by her family's immigration to the United States, Noah chose early to break cycles and claim her life with courage. Those choices fueled a decades-long journey of healing, service, and leadership that now touches audiences worldwide through her speaking, coaching, and the *World Healing Tour* podcast.

The Grass Grows Where I Am is a community project that gathers wise voices to remind us that meaning is here, where our feet are. Her work invites readers to soften the chase, befriend the present, and cultivate a grounded abundance. Noah helps people release comparison, competition, and scarcity so they can return to the truth already within them.

Noah's presence is deeply compassionate. She believes transformation begins when you tell the truth, honor your stories, and choose to live authentically, consciously, and with purpose. Noah lives this message daily with her family and community. Her greatest joy is helping you remember your light and share your gifts, creating ripple effects of healing wherever you go.

The grass doesn't grow greener somewhere else. The grass grows where you are, and Noah Crane is devoted to helping you see it, nurture it, and share it with the world.

Her message is simple and powerful: Together we are W-O-N; when one of us rises, all of us are lifted. Do your inner work and heal yourself, so you can heal the world.

Noah is blessed to be married to her soulmate Steven for over twenty-nine years. Together they have three beautiful children who they adore. Visit her at NoahCrane.com.

Leave a Review

Before you go, if you enjoy this book, will you please consider leaving a review on Amazon (or Barnes & Noble). As authors, there is nothing more that we appreciate than reading those reviews  from websites and Google from those of you who have found value, perspective, and ultimately joy from reading our book.

Thank you so much!

Made in the USA
Coppell, TX
05 February 2026